The Minister's Personal Guide

By
WALTER E. SCHUETTE

HARPER & BROTHERS, PUBLISHERS
New York

Library of Congress catalogue card number: 53–5448

To The Minister

The one great need in the Ministry, namely, maturity, cannot be provided by the theological seminary. Looking back, I see how unripe I was when I left the seminary to enter the calling which is so significant in the lives of men and women, and has such influence for good on communities and nations. When I finished college I was given a B.A.—Bachelor of Arts; and with it I entered the Ministry. It would have been more appropriate if the college had given me a B.W.—Babe in the Woods.

Now that I have lived long and learned at least a little, maybe I can help others learn more quickly and less painfully than I did. This does not, believe me, mean that I think I have learned it all—far from that. It is in sincere humility that I try to extend in the pages that follow, not criticism, but help to my fellow ministers.

WALTER E. SCHUETTE

Contents

CHAPTER 3: *The Minister's Home Life*

CHAPTER 4: *The Minister's Personal Affairs*

CHAPTER 5: *The Minister's Business Matters*

CHAPTER 6: *The Minister's Pastoral Relations*

CHAPTER 9: *The Minister's Moods*

The Minister's Personal Guide

Chapter 1

THE MINISTER'S CALL

1. WHEN THE MINISTER PROBES HIS CREDENTIALS

When, ages ago, one of our illustrious predecessors in the high calling of the Ministry stood with eyes protruding as he gazed stupefied at the mass of flapping, wriggling fish caught in his nets, a catch far outweighing any other in his long experience on Lake Gennesaret, the Man at whose command he had let down his nets said to him, "Henceforth thou shalt catch men." That was in the first century; we are living in the twentieth. But in no century has this Man, our Master, made higher claims upon his ministers than he makes on us today. No matter how complexly organized or how woefully demoralized the times may be, worldliness is still a sea from which souls must be lifted, if God's will is to be done. Still the commission sounds: "I will make you fishers of men—henceforth thou shalt catch men."

It must be emphasized that the gospel minister is God's workman. He must not be uncertain or timid about feeling and asserting that he is; nor must he be neglectful of giving good evidence of it. This century is not different from those that have gone before it from the beginning of human history. "The natural man receiveth not the things of the Spirit of God." No period in man's history has meekly accepted God's sovereignty. Long before our reckoning of time, a tempter said to an innocent woman, "Yea, hath God said?" And she and her mate began to doubt. Ages after, I hear sneering wicked King Ahab say to Elijah, God's accredited messenger, "Art thou he that troubleth Israel?" The minister must expect to have his God and his ambassadorship for God doubted—and flouted.

In apparent league with the world in its denial of his divine embassy, the minister's own heart sometimes inclines him to wonder whether he is actually sent by God. Is any man, whatever his talents, whatever his industry, worthy to be considered God's workman? Read the epic chapter in the Book of Job in which Job is asked to match himself with the strange creature of the deep called "Leviathan." He learns that though puny man stands helpless before forces and giants of nature, the Creator holds them all in the hollow of His hand. How much greater, then, must be the awe in which this man stands before the Creator!

How long it took God to convince the diffident Moses that he could serve as His ambassador! On the day of Peter's miraculous draft of fish, that rough-and-ready boatman stammered, "Depart from me; for I am a sinful man, O Lord." In your ministry, my Brother, I predict that you will again and again ask yourself whether it can actually be true that you are a workman by the grace and at the command of God.

This being the case, you will not accuse me of puerile naïveté because I lay first emphasis on the assertion that the minister is God's workman. To me, this is the basic consideration which enables him to follow his vocation, enthusiastic and unwearied. No lower conception of his calling is permissible. The treacheries and the hardships, the heartbreaks and the dyings, which he inevitably meets on his daily errands, cannot be manfully endured without this conviction. You may have wondered what great treasure was at stake when Paul penned his argument for his undeniable apostleship. He knew—and it made a world of difference to him as he encountered terrors so mighty, bore burdens so heavy, and endured discouragements so crushing, that no minister of his day or since could compare with him in his record.

Brother, God sends you into the Ministry. If not, you have no accrediting. You cannot bless or be blessed in the Ministry if you do not feel the hand of God's compulsion on you. Let us admit that there is loose talk in some circles about the "inner call." It is often indulged in by men who feel cocksure that they have direct wireless connection with heaven. In some of them it is a case of having gone "haywire." But their unreliability in the matter does not put the question, "Does God send you into the Ministry?" into the realm of the unanswerable. All you need is: First, the clear knowledge that God wants some men to be His ministers; second, the testimony of reliable friends and advisers as to your mental and physical fitness for the work; third, a conscience which tells you that the responsibility is yours. If, in addition to this, you feel that the Holy Spirit directly planted a conviction in your heart and mind that God wanted you personally in the ordained Ministry of the Church, well and good.

Conceiving that this has been your entrance into the Ministry, do not hesitate to lay claim, before others and in your own consciousness, to being God's emissary. This need not be done boastfully. The minister who boastfully parades himself makes me doubt that he is God's agent. There is the easy possibility of being confident, yet modest, in one's claim concerning himself. One walks then with firm tread, lifted carriage, and steady eye, showing the Ministry to be a delight no matter what comes or does not come; and at the same time an esprit which cautions the minister to place himself humbly under God's guidance in all that he thinks, says and does, and all that he leaves unthought, unsaid and undone.

2. When the Minister Receives a Definite Call

When a man decides to devote all that he is and has, for the entire period of his life, to the unique work of preaching the Gospel of the Cross of Jesus Christ in order to bring salvation to immortal souls; when he later accepts service through an organized church or congregation with attendant responsibilities to the community, it is a violation of all proper feeling to say that he has been hired. In all churches we speak of the minister's call—his original call into the Ministry itself, and of his periodic calls to serve specific groups.

Uncouth, though possibly well-meaning men will probably always speak of hiring a minister; and legally his written call to a local church and his acceptance of the call are classed as a contract. But the service he is to render is of such character as to lead thoughtful people, even those outside the church, to discuss it in terms different from those regularly employed when lay persons enter into agreements covering service to others.

Into a minister's keeping, people entrust the welfare of their immortal souls. Into his care they place the safeguarding of their children's souls. They make him a confidant in matters which they do not mention to their closest friends or confide to the dearest members of their own families. Surely, one cannot associate the word "hiring" with the making of a solemn covenant between a man that is to shepherd souls and the souls that he is to shepherd.

But what of a minister's salary? Should he enter such covenant on mere faith? Here the old-time interpretation of the minister's salary proves its validity. If a man with all the material needs agrees to give his full time for the spiritual service of a church, then this church should see to it that he is relieved entirely of the necessity of engaging in any other activity in order to provide a livelihood for himself and the wife and family he has an undisputed right to have. The circumstance that a man's call stipulates a material income for him does not in any degree rob it of its special standing as a call.

In preparation for his life work the man who feels called into the Ministry submits to education and training in college and theological seminary. As he nears the completion of the prescribed course, a call is sent to him. I was trained in a seminary by reverend professors whose firm opinion was that a theological graduate should without question or quibble accept the first call he received. That was many years ago; I cannot say that I disagree with them even today.

I fear there is a tendency among theological students to give far too much consideration to the material advantages and disadvantages connected with work in the fields to which they are called. Would not some other call yield more money? Do I want to go into a small town? Could I not be located near a university where I might do postgraduate work? What is the social status of the members of the church making the call? Will the girl I intend to marry want to live so far from her relatives? Will she agree to live in that old parsonage? Has this church bright prospects of numerical growth?

Young man, "He that loveth father or mother more than me is not worthy of me." "He that hath set his hand to the plow and looketh back . . . ." Maybe God wants you in that particular field because you need the experience which that field will give you. Maybe there is one soul in that field whose development into something great in the Kingdom needs just your ministry. It is a tragic thing to be laboring in God's Kingdom haunted by the thought, "Maybe God did not want me here." That thought cannot intrude to harass you if you accept the first call that reaches you.

What of calls received after one is settled in a parish? Few men are destined to labor in the same parish for years on end. The rule is change; and it is a wise one. Both pastor and congregation are likely to get into hopeless ruts if they remain together too long. Constituted and conditioned as we are, we need to encounter the demands which changes necessarily bring.

How should a settled pastor proceed when he receives a call? He may belong to a church body in which episcopal or conference appointments obtain. Then he has little choice. The pastor who has to make his own decision is not to be envied. The recipient of a call, unless he has been yearning for release from unwelcome conditions, is usually placed in an embarrassing situation.

Let earnest consideration guide him. When he is called from one parish to another he has, for the time, two alternatives: the call which has newly come to him and the call under which he accepted his present pastorate. Since both are valid and divine, which one is now meant for him? The congregation he is serving finds it easy to think only of its own advantage. The same holds true of the congregation which has now called him. It is for him to consider impartially the claims of each. Then, with selfless prayers for guidance, and after consultation with the officers of his church body and other experienced men, he reaches a decision.

If he decides that it is God's will for him to transfer to the new location, let him announce this to his people and ask them to grant him their dismission. If they urge him to remain and he cannot convince his mind (not his heart) that they are right, let him firmly resign and insist on the acceptance of his resignation. Under such circumstances few parishes will refuse.

On the other hand, if the pastor cannot reach a decision which leaves his mind at ease, let him place the case frankly and squarely before his parishioners, asking them to decide for him, and begging them not to allow considerations of personal attachment to control their votes. Their decision should be reached by ballot. If the votes strongly favor his remaining, he may in peace of mind continue where he is. If they are in favor of his release, or almost evenly divided, let him end his sojourn in that parish. The latter may result because the church members are convinced that the new field will offer him new advantages and they cannot begrudge him any improvement. However, the result of the ballot may indicate that he has not been filling the requirements. It is for him to do some serious self-examining, as he sadly takes his staff in hand to leave.

Once a decision to leave has been reached, let the minister be prompt about going. True, he is still pastor there; but his acceptance of the new call has worked a subtle change which will make the intervening efforts in his field almost uselessly applied. He need not feel that he is obligated to make a personal farewell call on every family in the parish. Lingering on the doorstep is usually wasted time. His new field probably needs him without delay.

3.   When the Minister Begins Work in a New Parish

No one seems oftener to ignore the significance of the old saw, "A new broom sweeps clean," than the minister who enters a new parish. There is another old saw which, if kept handy, might spare him many an ache and pain. It reads, "Be sure you're right, then go ahead"; and if "haste makes waste" applies anywhere, it is when a newly called minister is going through the inevitable adjustment period of his first months in a parish.

There are the lingering memory and affection entertained by many parishioners for his predecessor. The new man will hear kind words spoken of this minister and, when they refer to certain ways of doing things, the new minister is more than likely to infer that he is expected to adopt his predecessor's methods—or else. At once the flesh is raw; for, do not forget, the minister too is flesh. How quickly raw flesh quivers! How readily an unguarded tongue responds to the quivering!

There is the pride in itself which is inherent in every church, even the little old rural church, even the struggling city mission. When the new minister says, "Well, now, in my former parish we did this thus-and-so," he is at once on dangerous ground. No group of people with a little pride care to hear what they interpret to be invidious comparison of their methods with those of another similar group. There will be wags who remark, "If that parish was so perfect, why didn't he stay with it?"

There is the regrettable circumstance that in almost every parish a minister has his special friends and intimate consultants. The new minister, of course, wants to establish himself in the circle of the "right people" in his new field. But, now, every parish has "designing" members. They are lying in wait for the new minister. The former minister had found them out and was on his guard. The new minister had better be on his guard before he commits himself to any person or any group. He does not yet know who the "right people" are. By the way, it is usually unwise for any minister, new or old, to become very confidential with any of his church members. Not only is he likely to get into embarrassments by so doing, but it also hurts any church to have it known that there are privileged and underprivileged members in its group. News of this is sure to leak out.

Whatever a minister may think of making house calls on his members when there is no sickness or other happening to make such calls required, the new minister should, as soon after his arrival as possible, call at every home in the parish; and, since the man of the house is often absent through the day and not all calls can be made in the evening, the new minister should "drop in" at offices and places of business. The right kind of preaching, to be sure, will draw people's hearts to the minister; but no matter how much personality and heart approach his sermons may have, there is a friendly contact to be made in calls at homes and business places for which there is no adequate substitute. Members of a parish will in a degree be strangers to the minister until he has been their guest.

As the new minister endeavors to make himself acquainted with his people in their own daily surroundings, he will, if he is astute, as rapidly as possible make himself acquainted also with the organizations, methods, customs and trends of his new parish. Doing this, he will usually detect the desirability of changes. Wisdom decrees that, however much he may be astonished at some of the practices and neglects of his predecessor, changes of any kind, even minor changes, should be made cautiously and inconspicuously. Absence of any desire to gain credit for effecting improvements will help immeasurably. Many people, progressive though they be otherwise and elsewhere, are tradition-bound in their church conceptions. Changes in church management should develop gradually. The less notice such changes attract, the better for pastor and people.

Another exercise of wisdom on the new minister's part is the judicious concealment for a while of some of his talents and abilities. Church members like to discover as time goes on that "there is more to this minister" than was apparent on first acquaintance. It is also a mistake for any minister, when he enters a new parish, no matter how sure of himself he may be, to announce a (supposedly impressive) comprehensive program. If prudent, he will keep his plans to himself as much as possible, except as their development may require publicity. The minister who operates like leaven is happier in the work and invites fewer disappointments than he who works explosively. Feeling one's way is good strategy when one is in unfamiliar territory.

Many years ago, on an engagement in a large city church, my companion and I were confidently, not to say boastfully, informed by the comparatively new minister there: "I told my councilmen last week that having me would cost them plenty of money, because I intend to carry out a program which calls for extensive remodelling and additions to the buildings here." That minister is still there—so are the selfsame buildings, with not a single addition. He did not add an iota to his prestige by his cocky announcement, and probably has long since worn out his welcome.

These reflections must include the thought that a new minister should not at first set himself a pace which he cannot maintain. This applies to both his preaching and his pastoral activities. It may be true that first impressions concerning a minister signify a great deal; but first impressions should not exhibit a prospect which will soon fade from view. Putting best foot foremost does not mean striking a stride which cannot possibly be maintained. The minister who expends

all his energy in an eager attempt to impress his new parish,
and inevitably grows weary, need not expect much sympathy
from his friends.

4. WHEN THE MINISTER ARRANGES HIS DAILY SCHEDULE

In many people's minds the age-old opinion still sticks, that
the minister has comparatively little to do. The better he
preaches, the easier the average layman thinks it is for him.
The more neatly he dresses, the lighter his tasks seem to the
laboring man who cannot wear smart clothes every day, and
to the old-style housekeeper who is at all hours wearing an
apron and keeping her sleeves rolled up. One of the minister's
serious obligations to the high office which he occupies is to
prevent the spreading and deepening of the false notion that
he is a man of comfortable leisure. It is easy in any parish to be
lazy in the Ministry, at least for a time; but nowhere else is
indolence so unpardonable; and sooner or later it is certain to
inflict heavy punishment. Be it added that lazy ministers are
to be found; and they are largely responsible for the prevalence of the notion that the Ministry is a sinecure.

Also, some pastors are to blame for the recurrence of the old
quip that they spend too much time in bed. I used to drive
past a parsonage in which every day all the window shades
were still drawn down to the sills as late as eleven o'clock in
the forenoon. There was much talk about this. The minister's
published excuse for his late rising was that he burned midnight oil until three and four o'clock in the morning. This
excuse did not get general acceptance.

Absurd as is the charge that the minister has work on only
one day in the week, he can best combat the jibe by being an
early riser. It may seem true, as some ministers aver, that
there is far less disturbance and distraction after twelve o'clock
midnight than there is after seven o'clock in the morning; but
the early riser does not need so much quiet and calm to do
solid work in his study. He will gain much in various ways by

having it generally known that he does not stay abed late into the morning hours. Let me also venture the idea that sermons prepared by the light of midnight oil are likely to lack freshness and reality, smelling of oil even though kerosene has surrendered to electricity.

The day early grasped should be a day well planned, and he who admonishes his parishioners to do all in the name of the Lord, taking their concerns to Him in prayer, may well apply the admonition to himself. The first minutes of the day should find him in communion with his God. If he is at all acquainted with this God, he will know that such communion can be very real and satisfactorily helpful without his sitting for an hour or more in quiet meditation. Worshiping God in spirit and in truth can be honestly done while a man is dressing, shaving and breakfasting. Long and happily rewarding experience has made me a devotee of the practice of singing precious hymns for the half hour before breakfast. A lot of praying can be poured into every stanza of our great Christian hymns, and the morning program can be varied with the Church seasons. Thoughtful singing is a wonderful devotion.

Some ministers have, however, gone to strange lengths in their morning devotions. They have allowed themselves to be impressed by the philosophy that, if at the opening of the day a person will only fully relax, and sit, lie or stand motionless and blank-minded, God will grant him what is called guidance, giving him mental or volitional direction which will definitely schedule all his movements for the day. Fortunately, those who commit themselves to this persuasion sooner or later, usually sooner, discover that they are mistaken. No divine promise that God will do our thinking and planning for us is recorded anywhere. It is true that we are the clay and He is the Potter; but He has made it very plain that this does not mean that He will make our decisions for us, and that all we have to do is to be passively pliant.

Starting the day aright includes consideration of the minister's physical health. The average minister does not get enough of the right kind of muscular exercise. He should put himself through a daily regular program of physical culture if he is to be at his best physically, mentally and spiritually. I speak from experience. When I had been in the Ministry about ten years, I was a shallow-chested weakling. Something jolted me into the realization that I must do something about myself. Consulting neither physician nor athletic director, but reading here and there, I assembled a set of movements which I was convinced would develop and toughen every muscle in my frame. I put myself through these movements pitilessly morning and night. At this writing I have been in the Ministry over sixty-four years, having been in retirement one year, and am still doing a considerable amount of supply preaching. All along, my health has been marvelously preserved. For the last twenty-eight years of my service, I occupied a position which sent me traveling thousands of miles every year, by train, bus and automobile. To the last (just to illustrate) I had no difficulty in climbing in and out of upper Pullman berths without a ladder. Nobody can, for me, discount the value of a set of bodily exercises. I won a prize in one of Bernarr Macfadden's contests, and had my article and picture published in *Physical Culture*. I know that, in the first years of my ministry, more than one kind lady sighed, "Poor boy, he'll not live long."

The day's first meal deserves consideration. There was for a while a theory that, after one's tissues had been renewed by a night's sleep, no food was needed at the beginning of the day. This clashed with another flatly contradictory theory. I think the sensible view is that a minister needs only a light breakfast. Were he to do manual labor in field or mill, he would need a substantial hunger appeasement to stand by him until noon. But, even when his morning's work is not sedentary, it is as a rule not such as to make heavy demands on his physical resources.

Dietitians have traveled far since the days when people, ministers among them, chewed buckwheat cakes and flannel cakes and hot bread into wads, and transferred them, oiled with syrup, to their stomachs, to lie there as indigestible boluses. The minister, who may pooh-pooh many of the dietitian's warnings, will do well to heed his advice as to breakfast.

Days are not alike. The weather at daybreak varies greatly. There are far too many people who begin the day with growls about the fog, the heat, the rain, the snow, the humidity, the raw wind. The minister, who is a special servant of the God who decrees the weather, will do well to refrain from finding fault with it and with Him at the opening of the day. A cheerful, optimistic spirit should be his; the spirit which is ascendant in him when he begins a day is of particular importance in his calling. Least of all is he justified, when a Sunday opens with every indication that the weather will ruin the church attendance, in letting it so affect him that his conduct of the service betrays that he himself is a "weather Christian." Often, when an audience is small, the miraculous happens. The minister must not hinder it.

The minister's morning toilet deserves consideration. I ask him to shave every day without exception, preferably early in the morning. I also ask him to dress carefully early in the morning. He should be carefully dressed always, unless he occasionally needs to don old clothes or overalls to do rough manual work. It is not beneath the minister's dignity to garden, to tend his own lawn, shrubs and trees, to tinker with his automobile, to do odd jobs in house, attic and cellar. But addiction to such activities should not become a ruling passion with him, and he should not display himself in dishabille. Church members are not favorably impressed when they see their minister in all sorts of undress, wearing old slippers, lopping about collarless, even shirtless, hair unkempt. I knew a minister who answered his front door bell in his stocking feet.

What about the morning newspaper? Well, it may be best to read it early and have that done for the day. There is little to reward the minister for giving the daily newspaper close and comprehensive attention. Most of its contents are not worth the time it takes to read them. Just the same, the minister dare not let the events of the day escape his notice. He is expected to be acquainted with world events and community doings, and all the happenings that lie between. Time (not too much) bestowed on the morning newspaper is time fairly well invested.

But, supposing the day to be properly begun, what of the day itself? An effectual way of warding off the charge that the minister leads a lazy life, as also to avert the likelihood of slipping into aimlessness and indolence, is to fix a fairly inflexible daily and weekly schedule. To be sure, the conglomerate demands made on the Ministry in our times render such technique quite difficult. Hours allotted for study are unceremoniously broken into by some parishioner, who telephones that the minister is wanted immediately. An impressive voice asks him whether he does not know that So-and-So is very "low." Often the reportedly afflicted member has nothing more serious than a common cold and is not even abed. I remember visiting a man who, I had been notified, was quite ill. True, I found him in bed; but only because, as was the good old Southern custom, he had taken his periodic dose of calomel. That certainly makes a man sick; but the sickness is not one that calls for the minister's prayers and the interruption of his work schedule.

Howbeit, whatever rough sailing a well-planned work schedule may frequently encounter, it is worth trying to preserve. It is also worth publicizing and defending: so many and such hours a day for reading, study, research, preparation of the sermon and the Sunday School lesson; for pastoral calling, giving precedence to calls on the sick; for recreation (just as necessary as the other departments of the minister's activity); and for sleep. Once a parish learns that its pastor has as regular a schedule as the man in the store, the office or the shop, and that he is positively minded to "punch the clock" in maintaining his schedule, the members will gradually grow to respect their minister's time, and most of them will observe the rules.

A frequent disturber of his work program is the minister's wife. Be it admitted that she has a perfect right to expect him to assist in the running of the household routine. The parsonage loses much of its charm, and the minister forfeits a large portion of the blessedness of a wife's companionship, when she is left to struggle with all the domestic requirements without his aid. Granted that she is the one to do the dishes, to tidy the rooms, to make the beds, she is not the one to bring in coal and wood, carry out the ashes, clean the automobile, mow the lawn and fire the furnace.

The question is not solved by insisting that the parsonage should have a competent maid and a handy yard man. Few ministers can afford such services. More than that, there are few maids and yard men who will not carry all sorts of gossip from the parsonage out into the parish: gossip which, often half-truth, will prove annoying and even destructive.

I think hundreds of ministers will bear me out in the assertion that one can keep his mind actively studying while he is doing the usual physical labor of house, yard and garden. One need not be neglecting the sacred duties of the minister's high calling while he rubs up the car or pushes the lawn mower. Make choretime a study period. But, returning to the wife, let the minister firmly have her understand that she must not, for all sorts of things, infringe on his time.

If the minister's voluntary daily program should be kept inviolable, his schedule of appointments and services and meetings should be even more binding. It is inexcusable for him to be late for any appointment he has made, or for any service or meeting. Ten thirty should never mean ten thirty-five on Sunday mornings, and eight should not mean eight fifteen in any evening. Punctuality is one of his musts.

5. WHEN THE MINISTER HAS SERVED THE SAME PARISH
MANY YEARS

The relation between a pastor and the members of his congregation is unlike any other human relationship. It is a
peculiarly delightful one. A pastor goes to a congregation and
immediately, without further ceremony, his official and social
standing is established. His personal relation to all the individual members of the flock begins auspiciously; and, day
by day, year by year, in joys and in sorrows, this relation
grows; and by and by it is something incalculably precious.
How long can, how long should, it continue? Is it advisable,
is it safe, for the minister to remain in the same parish so long
that he becomes a patriarch?

I have often advised pastors to begin wondering about
continuing in the same parish after they have shepherded it
five years; to think of a transfer after ten years; and to consider this definitely, seriously, after fifteen years. This does not
mean that a longer stay is inescapably ruinous. There will
always be perfectly happy celebrations of twentieth and
twenty-fifth installation anniversaries. It means only that there
are many considerations which make it best not to extend one
pastorate much beyond fifteen years. Some church communions have simplified the solution of the problem through the
episcopal or the Conference system of appointments and
transfers, with a time limit. This, however, as is well known,
opens the door to various undesirable experiences which do
not make for the welfare of the church. But, even when the
minister can rely on the continuance of his appointment, the
question of the long pastorate needs careful study.

As one serves a parish, little unpleasant affairs between
pastor and parishioner inevitably occur. They come—and apparently go. Just the same, each one leaves its mark; and, as
the years accumulate, these little frictions and the heat they
generate also accumulate. Eventually, without being able to
lay finger on any specific charge against the minister, even his

most loyal friends and supporters in the parish are forced to admit to themselves that the pastor has worn out his welcome, perhaps without one serious fault on his part.

In most cases, I suppose, this testimony, "without one serious fault on his part," would in all honesty have to be omitted. Every pastor (except you, Brother) has peculiarities. Few pastors rid themselves of them, but rather let them multiply. Pulpit mannerisms, social practices, pet expressions, vagaries in dress, decrease of effort (which is equivalent to increase of neglect), or inclinations in various queer directions—constant exposure to these gradually wears on the patience and good will of church members. The younger are more critical than the older. Ultimately, the members and the pastor are no longer knit together as they should be, except outwardly. Yes, he has worn out his welcome.

Maturity is a priceless acquisition of the experienced minister; but I fear the average minister's maturity gravitates strongly in the direction of self-satisfaction. Perhaps unavoidably, by reason of fallible human nature, he loses his freshness, grows stale, to say it bluntly; and, instead of remaining the industrious self-examining man he should constantly be, he takes himself or his standing for granted. This is, emphatically, not good; and the best recommended cure is a transfer to another parish, where he will be compelled to prove again certain things which he had considered firmly established.

Few ministers seem to have the insight to realize that the children whom they have baptized, instructed and confirmed are no longer children after they have reached their upper teens and have had away-from-home contacts. They still love the minister and cherish memories of his gracious attentions to them; but this does not divest them of the feeling that, somehow, he is not measuring up to the requirements of a new day. They have grown, the world has moved, he has stood still. He needs an elixir. Will he take it unless he is called into a new field?

We hear it said that Pastor So-and-So has got into a rut.

Well, he probably has. But it is just as true that his overlong service in the same parish has allowed it to get into a rut also. Not so good—pastor and parish in a rut! Can they possibly make the speed and exhibit the efficiency which the times demand?

There is another side to the subject. Ministers have different gifts. In most ministers, one or two abilities stand out. I raise these questions: Is it fair to let one parish for years on end enjoy certain abilities which its minister possesses? Should it not share him with some other parish? Why not pass the good things around? And may not this parish have been deprived all these years of certain other abilities which its minister did not have, which a new minister would have supplied?

Still another side: as the minister who remains too long gradually begins to take things for granted, so the members of his parish follow the same gravitation. The minister is satisfied—why worry? Much as they love him, they are overlooking many an exercise which a parish owes its minister and without which he is not at his best.

I venture to say that few congregations in which a minister has served a long term of years are fully satisfied. Do not let appearances deceive you. Your people may act as though they think all is well. They may even, if you receive a call elsewhere, pass a dutiful resolution asking you to remain with them. All the while, down in their hearts and up in their minds, they may be realizing that a change would be best for them and for you. Better not decline that call without doing some deep-sea sounding to discover the actual state of affairs.

But, suppose that all is indisputably going well. Listen. Is it not better to leave when this is true, than to wait until you are compelled to leave because something has gone wrong?

Chapter 2

THE MINISTER'S OFFICIAL RELATIONS

1. WHEN THE MINISTER CONDUCTS A SUNDAY SERVICE

Does the average minister realize that from the moment he appears before his Sunday audience to the very close of the service he is under unremitting and, with some of his audience, merciless surveillance?

This audience is a peculiar complex. The devout are there, who consider an hour spent in the church service an hour spent very close to God Almighty. A few school children and youths are there, who quickly notice mispronunciations; some high school pupils also, who know whether the preacher's diction is good or poor. The witty are there, who see straight through pretentions of showmanship, and the thoughtful, who want his reading and prayer to display insight and sincerity. No part of the service which the minister has to render permits him to be careless.

His posture as he sits on the platform or in the chancel attracts attention. People notice him when he lolls back in his chair and rests his right foot on his left knee, or vice versa. They wonder why he has to grasp the lectern and the pulpit, as it were for support, when he reads the lessons or delivers the sermon. They wonder why he keeps looking here and there in the audience while the hymns are being sung. On the other hand, they wonder why he does not look them in the face and in the eyes while he is preaching to (at?) them, but, instead, looks at the ceiling, or at the side wall, or at a remote point in the rear.

Whether one's church is liturgical or nonliturgical, it is quite generally accepted that the service is a holy service and that it should be conducted reverently. "The Lord is in His holy temple: let all the earth keep silence before Him." And let the minister lead in cultivating that reverence which is implied in the enjoined silence. For most people the church is no longer merely a meeting house.

The trend among Protestants toward decorum and proper ministerial dress in the house of God has greatly increased. The conservatives in the sixteenth-century Reformation retained much of the ritual and vestiture of the ancient Church. The extremists rejected it all, to the point of absurd iconoclasm. Today in many denominations in which ritual had been condemned the tendency is back again to form and parament. Naturally, the outward compliance precedes the ministerial esthetic feeling, and we find preachers officiating in robes which are fine and worthy, but in tan shoes, varicolored shirts and collars, protruding trouser legs of all shades, to make the robes look ridiculous. Even in churches which have all along been ritualistic there is much inexcusable carelessness in this regard. Get the feeling, Brother, and look to the details.

Most Sunday services include the reading of some portion of Scripture. Yet few ministers pay enough attention to good, effective, impressive reading. Some treat Scripture reading merely as a necessary filler, and the result is in accordance. Others read the Scripture as though ignoramuses were listening and they must add all sorts of inflections and emphases to make the Bible seem genuine. Real elocution, in some ministers' minds, is only a fad. They forget that the finest food can be made unpalatable, not to say indigestible, by slipshod serving. God's Word can be made distasteful and unsatisfying by incompetent reading.

A long section might be written about public prayer. Let the publicly praying minister bear in mind that God does not need a lot of detailed information; that at best it is difficult for worshipers to follow a spoken prayer and make it their own; and that, the longer he spins his prayer, the more certainly he destroys its benefit as far as his hearers, including God, are concerned. Most ministers whom I have heard in extemporaneous prayer would have done far better if they had read a well-thought-out prayer. But, again, the printed prayer can lose most of its beauty and effect if it is carelessly read, or even clumsily stumbled through, as is likely to be the case when the minister has not made himself familiar with its content and forgets that he should be approaching God with it in his heart.

In some small churches it seems necessary for the minister to lead in the singing of the hymns. In most churches this is unnecessary. The minister may very properly join in the singing of all the hymns, but, let me emphasize, not lustily, or so as to make the impression that singing is to be by main strength. In churches where responsive singing obtains in the liturgy he should strictly avoid uniting in the responses intended for the congregation. I have heard ministers say, "The Lord be with you," and then join vehemently in the congregation's response, "And with thy spirit!" Responsive services need much more study and consequent comprehension than many ministers accord to them.

In my seminary days, when all sorts of social doings were taboo, one of our most dignified instructors said, one day in class, that he wished every student preparing for the Ministry could take a dancing course. That professor had five children, and not one of them was ever seen on a dance floor; but he expressed himself as he did because he deplored the lack of grace and rhythm in the movements of many budding ministers when they conducted chapel services. There is no excuse for clumsiness when a man ministers in holy things. The grace of God should make him graceful. But overdone nicety of deportment is frequently worse than boorish clumsiness. Often unpreparedness is the cause of the minister's awkward movements. He fumbles for hymns and for Scripture readings because he has not selected and marked them beforehand. He reads the propers for the wrong Sunday because he has gone into the service without noting the Sunday.

Abhorring anything and everything in the minister's movements while he is conducting a divine service which would mark him as being on parade, I nevertheless like to have his movements conform to certain aesthetic expectations. I like to see him make smooth square turns when he moves from place to place in the sanctuary, from altar to lectern, from lectern to pulpit; and I like to have him stand erect, not needing anything on which to lean for support. I like to see him, if he must use his handkerchief, do it very unostentatiously. If he is speaking without vestments, I do wish that he would keep his hands out of his pockets, both vest and trousers, and his thumbs out of the armpits of his vest. I like to have all his movements unhurried: let him acquire and display poise. If he must leave the chancel or the platform after he has taken his place there for the opening service, let him make his exit and his re-entrance inconspicuous. If he joins in the choir processional and recessional, let him learn to march in and out erect, and in dignified gait.

Few ministers find the happy medium when they greet the members of their audience at the door at the close of the service. Some are stiff, and they go through the ordeal (that is what it is) as though bored. Others are so effusive and indulge in pleasantries so jocular that it looks as though they are glad to get away from an oppressive atmosphere of serious devotion and back into the hello and titter of the world and the worldly. Back slapping is nowhere in order, least of all in the church vestibule. And, while I am at this, let me say, "Preacher, don't paw people, especially women!" It appears suggestive and it is not welcomed, even when it is overlooked.

When, as sometimes happens, there is a disturbance in the auditorium or outside loud enough to attract attention, let the minister refrain from taking notice. Latecomers should not be

subjected to a stare from him. Restless children, even crying
infants, should not unnerve him, or draw his attention. To
assist him in preserving *sang-froid* under all provocations, the
ushers or deacons or elders should be alert to pay prompt and
deft attention to anything which may tend to interfere with
the smooth procedure of the service.

Confidence in the effectiveness of any liturgical form (*opus
operatum*) is rightly discountenanced by Protestants. Slavish
subservience in church matters is likewise unwelcome in our
liberty-loving atmosphere. Yet, when one belongs to a church
group which has adopted a fixed liturgical form of the public
service, one is duty-bound to adhere to the said form. I belong
to a liturgical church, and I have had supervision over two
hundred local congregations. My duties have quite often included the conduct of portions and sometimes of all of a
Sunday service. Invariably, I am compelled to inquire what
deviations from the prescribed form are customary in the
church I am visiting. These deviations are so usual and so
various as to make one exasperated, especially since there is
never a valid reason for them, often only the whim of the local
pastor. Most of them are so utterly without rhyme or reason
that again and again I am simply amazed. It has seemed to
me that a severe reprimand for the offending minister would
be about the only advisable proceeding. But—we are democratic and liberty-loving, and a reprimand would be resented—also be ineffectual.

Liturgical forms have been painstakingly, artistically and
thoughtfully built up. Many of them have the sanction of ages.
Their different parts and the sequence of these parts mean
something. Poor judgment is usually at work when they are
amended by the individual minister. I grant that among
professional liturgists there have been and still are extreme
enthusiasts; and often, when they are asked for a logical explanation of this and that form, their only answer is, "It is
liturgical." But, after all, the accumulation of the experience
and thought of generations of liturgists demands respect.

One of the strong arguments for a fixed liturgy is that members of one's denomination, visiting in other churches of their own denomination, will readily feel at home when they find exactly the same form of service in use there. Deviations from the accepted form disturb the visiting member and make him wonder; and a liturgy which disturbs has almost forfeited its right to the name.

2.   WHEN THE MINISTER IS IN THE PULPIT

Manifestly, this treatise cannot concern itself with the content and the form of his sermons, except to say that he is in that pulpit to proclaim the most important truths it is given to humanity to hear. It is for this reason that the impressions he makes as he delivers his messages are of great concern. These impressions, the average church audience being what it is, are dependent largely on the minister's conduct while he preaches. Pulpit mannerisms are so insidious that I have never known a preacher who was entirely free of them. They cannot be laughed off as being harmless. They serve no good purpose; and, once they interfere, as they invariably will, with the effect of the sermon on any hearer, they have become a menace.

List some of them as they are known to you: leaning on the pulpit; pounding the Bible; fingering the Bible pages or the pulpit paraments; throwing the pressure of one's abdomen on the edge of the Bible or the desk; getting on tiptoes (floor pressing), a favorite expedient of the preacher who is short in stature; clutching the pulpit edge, and thereby crushing the parament; using one's handkerchief like a mop on hands or forehead; dropping one's voice to a whisper for effect; putting one's hands or, even worse, one's thumbs into trouser or coat pockets; taking one's glasses off and putting them on repeatedly; using pet phrases over and over again; keeping one's eyes elsewhere than on one's audience; crouching, with knees bent, as if to make a spring; "making faces."

This is a long list, and it can easily be made longer. Some of its items deserve particular attention. For instance, the amazing habit of putting hands in pockets. Doing this is not permissible in ordinary polite society. If you cannot otherwise overcome this unattractive habit, have your wife take safety pins and make the pockets inaccessible on Sundays. What to do with your hands when you have no pulpit or lectern before you on which to let them repose? Why not stand up like a man and have your arms and hands down at your sides? Arduous? The soldier learns to drill and to hold all sorts of postures without complaining. If it is a terrible hardship to have your arms down at your sides, let us apply Paul's admonition, "Endure hardness, as a good soldier of Jesus Christ."

You need someone to keep you under constant observation and frankly call your attention to your too frequent use of pet phrases, gestures and postures. Maybe this could be your wife. But I have taken note of an adoration so prevalent among ministers' wives that I take little stock in their criticisms of their husbands. I think that the average parsonage couple are under the impression that they must constantly be on the defensive; for this cause the minister's wife shields him from her own detection of his failings. It is a case of "Poor Papa!"—but it is a sad mistake.

Most mannerisms are the product of a lack of poise. I do not mean a lack of self-confidence. The average minister has entirely too much of the latter. But few ministers cultivate poise; and it is one of the prize accomplishments for which to strive. The minister who has poise has the ability to keep his mind on himself, his appearance and his movements while on the platform or in the pulpit. Observers say, "How easy it is for him to speak." They do not comprehend how many weary efforts he has made to gain the poise which delights and mystifies his audiences.

How many ministers when they preach are careful enough of their diction and pronunciation? How many of them reflect that their failure to speak correctly and vitally is due to their own carelessness? How many of them are deeply enough concerned about captivating, gripping, their audiences? The preacher who attracts is the preacher who finds things to say and says them in ways which not every other minister finds and acquires.

3.   WHEN THE MINISTER MAKES PUBLIC ANNOUNCEMENTS

Liturgists claim that there is no proper place for announcements in the program of a divine service. One need not have a fully developed liturgical appreciation to catch the sense of their objections. To open a solemn service in the name of the Triune God, to continue it with prayer and Scripture reading and holy song, then to introduce the announcement of a strawberry festival, or a hayride party, or a basket picnic, is, if one has aesthetic feelings even in only a mild degree, malapropos (the liturgist would say sacrilegious, I suppose).

There was a time, before the prevalence of daily newspapers and weekly church bulletins, when there may have been justification for using the pulpit or the platform in the church for public notices. That time belonged to another generation. But we still have the minister who, in spite of publication in the local newspaper and in the Sunday church bulletin, fears that, unless he will with his own voice emphasize a notice, it will not be heeded. I grant that many church members remain in blissful ignorance after reading the plainest announcements; but this ignorance is by no means dispelled by a vocal announcement in the service.

We also have the minister who spins out announcements almost endlessly. Why can he not, if he is incurably addicted to the announcement habit, at least make his notices plain and terse? Does he imagine he makes a good impression by his "much speaking"?

Some have suggested that after the close of the service the audience be seated and remain for the announcements. This, it seems to me, simply transfers them from the category of interference to that of anticlimax. There should, if a service has fulfilled its purpose, be a certain fervor of devotion in people's minds as they leave God's house. The last moment should not be given over to a variety of lesser impressions.

The only rightful place for them is the printed bulletin. Where the minister is, by force of circumstances beyond his control, compelled to insert them into the devotional parts of the service, let him rob them as much as possible of their incongruity, number and dimension. When he accepts announcements, let him, unabashed, show his reluctance.

4. WHEN THE MINISTER SINGS IN CHURCH

It does not make much difference in the big and well-equipped church whether the minister has musical taste and ability or not; but more and more smaller churches are asking, when they choose a new minister, how much the man under consideration knows about music. Most ministers of my acquaintance have left the seminary with a fair knowledge of music, ability to play some musical instrument, or an average singing voice. Two theological seminaries used regularly to send me lists of the students about to be graduated, with sketches of their scholarship standing, their inclinations, and their accomplishments. Invariably mention was made of each student's status as to music.

Most congregations expect the minister to join in the singing of the hymns in the public service. It would look strange, indeed, were the minister to say, "Let us sing hymn number so-and-so," and then sit mute during the hymn singing. But I think it jars the average worshiper to have the minister sing lustily. Decorum should dictate that he remain inconspicuous as a singer in the public service. There may be a few small churches in which he is expected to add the functions of a precentor to his other duties; but the average congregation should be impressed with the duty to do its own singing.

Shall the minister be choir instructor and leader? One may

well be surprised at the number of churches in which he is so engaged. When this arrangement becomes necessary or desirable, let him drill the choir so that it can do its part at the Sunday service without having him in front of it waving his arms, or a baton. It is disturbing to see a minister, like a Jack-of-all-trades, bob from chancel or pulpit to choir loft and back again. Usually the choir which cannot render an anthem without the minister's assistance is not much of an asset. I have a sneaking suspicion that some ministers parade as choir directors to satisfy their own vanity.

To digress, let me add that a choir's part in the holy service is immeasurably depreciated by the visible presence of a director. The anthem should be an act of sincere worship. When a gesticulating director enters the scene, usually as the most prominent feature, the anthem becomes a performance. We do not go to church to see anybody perform. A choir can, when it sings sincerely and well, lift the souls of the worshipers to exalted heights; but the choirs which do this are few and far between. Let me admit that, much as I love music, in my opinion the average church choir is neither musically able nor devotionally uplifting.

5.   When the Minister Conducts a Funeral Service

Somehow, in most circles, no matter what the social standing of the deceased, no matter on which side of the railroad tracks death strikes, a minister is wanted at the funeral. He is called upon by so varied a group that he may well feel the need of earnest efforts to conduct himself discreetly and helpfully at the burial service. Not only do the circumstances under which death comes and the social and cultural standing of the households vary exceedingly, but so do the ideas of people on what the officiating minister should say and do, or leave unsaid and undone. Expectations and demands are often embarrassingly queer and exacting.

Some ministers solve all their funeral problems by assuming a dictatorial attitude, doing as they see fit and allowing no one else to make suggestions. Others go to the opposite extreme of complying with every wish and whim of the mourning family. A few may go so far as to become "ambulance chasers," virtually thrusting themselves in the role of the "officiating clergyman."

This chapter cannot claim to solve all the perplexing problems which confront the minister when he is to serve where death has entered a home. Let us first consider why the minister is at the funeral at all. For some people he is there only to enable them to observe propriety. So arresting does any death still seem, and so universal is the custom of disposing of the bodies of the dead to the accompaniment of some ritual form, that most people, even those who resort to cremation, feel under compulsion to have a religious funeral ceremony of some kind.

But the original custom of funeral services and of the special functioning of the minister when a dead body was to be laid away was based on thoughtful considerations. Very few human beings can evade the conviction that death does not end all. There must be a life beyond; and the soul of the dead has gone into yonder existence. More than that, even those who do not believe in the restoration of the body after death somehow have the impression that the body which is left after the departure of the soul cannot be treated simply as "the remains."

Christian believers, followers of Him who said, "I am the Resurrection and the Life," convinced of the reality of the life of the soul after it has left the body, as also of the coming resurrection of the body, see in the procedure of the reverent disposition of the dead body an occasion for solemnization; and nothing can be more logical than the officiating of a Christian minister. The minister's attitude throughout, then, must be determined by his understanding that he is to solemnize the occasion.

This cannot be done either by taking a dictatorial, managerial position or by a complacent yielding to all sorts of demands on the part of the bereaved. The minister must learn to strike a course which lies between the two extremes. If his heart is truly evangelistically sympathetic in the Christian sense of these terms, and if his desire to lead souls near to Christ in the presence of death is genuine and earnest, he will probably avoid serious mistakes; although, to be sure, he cannot expect to avoid unfavorable criticism.

The presence of human death creates an atmosphere in which it is possible and proper to impress solemn warnings on the careless and the indifferent, even on the hardened sophisticates; but it does not set a stage on which it is prudent for the minister to administer stinging rebukes. The presence of human death does call for the application of healing balm to stricken hearts; but the minister who derives satisfaction from bringing tears to eyes and wringing sobs from throats should not delude himself into thinking that he has thus healed and soothed, even though some who are present will give him credit for having shown deep sympathy for the sorrowing. Nor should he imagine that fulsome praise of the departed is a real solace to the bereaved.

Tributes to the deserving are not out of place at their funerals; but such tributes should be temperate, and they must not displace in the minister's funeral message the comforting gospel truth which is so much more important. Discreetly sparing reference to the life of the departed, avoidance of extravagant eulogy, are not only in better taste than their opposites, but they may save the minister many an embarrassing experience. Who knows how soon he may be officiating at the funeral of someone whom he cannot conscientiously or intelligently praise so lavishly, but whose relatives will dislike him if he does not?

The minister's funeral sermon begins before the day of the burial. There is the opportunity of a blessed ministry beckoning to him when death has entered a household and the members of this household are passing through an experience which, even though it may not be new to them, somehow awes their minds and awakens in them longings which appreciate the inadequacy of all earthly things. Let the minister go into the bereaved home after deep thought on what he may be able to say in answer to the inevitable questions which arise on such occasions, and what he may employ to impart true comfort.

Years ago there was much argument of the question as to who was to have a Christian burial, and who not. Now, in exact reality there is no such thing as a Christian burial. Laying a dead body into the ground and covering it with earth is not a religious act. The question should have been, "At whose funeral should a Christian pastor function?" I believe a thoughtful mind will reach the conclusion that the activity of a Christian pastor is always in order, and that he has no right to refuse to build the Kingdom anywhere. He has a right at various funerals to disappoint the expectations of people who look to him to act the hypocrite. When he is asked to serve at burials of persons who to his certain knowledge were evidently grossly irreligious or flagrantly immoral, he may very properly inform those who request his service that he will not be able to extend them comfort in regard to their dead, but that he is willing to be with them and to announce God's blessed truth to them. If they agree to be satisfied with what he can conscientiously do, all will be well. I am here tempted to deliver myself in regard to the clergy who have officiated at the gaudy obsequies of men prominent in the underworld, notorious gamblers, vicious gunmen, and their ilk—but I refrain.

It has gradually come to pass that undertakers (Is it politer to say morticians or funeral directors?) have assumed the ordering not only of the external arrangements for burials, but also of the minister's part in the service; and this inclination on the part of undertakers has sometimes reached the stage of actual interference with the minister's plans. It is time to call a halt in this respect. Undertakers are very useful men in their line, and most of them co-operate very agreeably with the clergy, but the minister does not need or want their selection of what he is to read and say.

At many funerals today there is no address, no oration. The preacher reads a series of Bible verses, some poetry and some prayers. He does not therewith live up to his opportunities. It does not take a trained, highly educated, ordained minister to do a little reading. If the minister has no heart message for the souls attending a burial, why is he there? Is he merely ornamental, conventional?

Perhaps the funeral address is frowned upon by undertakers and others because some preachers make it entirely too long and wearisome. I have no defense for the long-winded preacher. But his transgressions should not determine that no minister shall henceforth bear a helpful message to the persons assembled for a burial. This message can be made deeply important, heart-searching and heart-healing, without extending itself over a period of many minutes; and this is precisely what it should be.

Is it necessary to say a few words about the minister's attire at a funeral service? I fear it is. There are still clergymen, either so intent on keeping themselves comfortably cool in hot weather, or so ill informed as to the proprieties, that they conduct funeral services in Palm Beach suits and other informal outfits. Clothes do not make a man, but clothes can catalogue a man as a boor.

Whether or not to read an obituary at a funeral service should be left to the wishes of the bereaved family; but, if one is read, the minister should so compose or edit it that it does not contain all sorts of petty details. If those who are "left to mourn their loss" are listed, I have always argued that the names of the in-laws should not be included; nor should the list end with "a host of acquaintances and friends." Let these be taken for granted. It is true that the dead has left them; but he or she has also, by departing this life, left another two and one-half billion fellow men on earth.

I cannot join the chorus of ministers who protest against certain songs often used at funerals. If John, in Revelation, was authorized to rhapsodize about a river clear as crystal, and about trees which bore twelve manner of fruits and new fruit every month, and about a city which had walls studded with twelve kinds of gems, whose gates were pearls, whose streets were pure gold, why dare we not sing about a "beautiful isle of somewhere"? After all, the only thing we know about the location of heaven is that it is "somewhere."

Similarly, I cannot add my voice to the protests often entered by ministers against the sending of floral tributes. There is a language which can best be spoken by flowers sent in loving memory or sympathy. It is by no means a waste of money to express one's feelings through beautiful and fragrant blossoms. Notifying the bereaved that one has given three dollars (or less?) to foreign missions or some other good cause instead of sending flowers is to me a strange procedure which, I believe, originated somewhere in Europe. It is equivalent, when analyzed, to saying, "Since your dear one died, I am giving some benevolence money which the benevolence treasurer would not otherwise have got out of me." Let people give their gifts to foreign missions without needing the prod of someone's death; and let them at the same time help brighten the gloom this death has brought by sending the flowers also. (N.B. The Florists' Association is not paying me for this notice.)

As soon as possible after the day of the funeral the minister should call at the bereaved home. I do not believe that many will accuse him of calling in order to collect a fee. Special attention at such times is not only Christian: it may be a means of real evangelizing. Death raises many questions in the minds of even thoughtless people when it invades their family circle; and, somehow, the minister knows the answers to these questions, does he not? The very fact that he exhibits sincere concern may open doors which usually are closed or only slightly ajar.

6. WHEN THE MINISTER CALLS ON THE SICK

Contrary to some people's ideas, calling on the sick is one
of the minister's most difficult and perplexing responsibilities.
This is all the more disquieting because there is nothing more
important on the pastor's schedule than his ministry to the
sick. "The sick" can be made a generic term; and a pastor's
visits to the sick can, in consequence, be made a routine,
stereotyped performance, even a perfunctory activity. I fear
few pastors take pains to consider each afflicted person an
individual case. That is one reason why the professional
psychiatrist is supplanting the consecrated gospel minister at
bedsides in sickrooms.

To make a special study of each patient in one's parish, taking into consideration his or her background, age, tem-
perament, disposition, religious experience or inexperience,
connections with family and with friends, and allowing all
these items to figure in making an estimate of the patient's
reactions and reflections under the burden of sickness, does
not catalogue a minister's visits to the sick among the easy
tasks of his varied round. But satisfying results cannot be
registered without all this, and the minister who conscientiously applies himself to the proper evaluation of these items
before he visits will eventually surprise himself as having
become a fairly good psychiatrist, plus being the bearer of
God's comfort.

His study of cases and persons must not, to be sure, be
devoid of a genuinely sympathetic interest in the patient and
his or her alleviation. It is herein that the devoted minister
can often far outshine a professional psychiatrist. His heart is
in his efforts to comfort and uplift the ailing. After all, it is
the heart that needs comfort and uplift when one is sick; and
only another heart can really aid a burdened one.

One of the perplexing elements in the visitation of the sick
by the pastor is the prevailing impression that death is cer-

tainly near when one is sick enough to make the pastor feel obliged to call. How frequently members of the family of a seriously sick person, who ask the minister to call, solemnly try to pledge the minister to pretend when he arrives that he just "dropped in" by chance. In plain terms, the minister is told that he cannot be a real friend and helper unless he acts the hypocrite. Ministers, especially inexperienced ones, often accede to this request. They come breezing in as though by chance, express astonishment at finding someone of the household sick, and, of course, under the circumstances cannot bear any burden of the seriousness of the situation.

Most ministers will probably confess that they have often been in doubt whether or not to offer prayer for the sick. A young fellow is lying seriously diseased. The minister fears that, if he makes the young man's condition seem grave enough to call for special prayer, the young fellow may tell the family not to admit him again. "Does he think I'm going to die?" It is in such cases that the minister's careful advance study of the patient's situation and his probable state of mind may save the day by guiding him to enter so adroitly into the boy's regard and confidence that prayer for him, or with him, takes place naturally and makes him want the call repeated.

I think that sometimes it is wiser to advise the sick one not to forget to pray and to put his trust in the Great Physician than for the minister to do the praying. Anyhow, is it not about time to convince our people that the minister's prayers do not have especially effectual virtue, and that their own prayers may please the Heavenly Father more? We Protestant clergy prate a great deal about every soul's having free access to God without the mediation of priests.

One of the minister's distressing dilemmas occurs when he is in the room of a member who is pretending to be ill. What kind of praying shall he do, for example, for one who wants to frighten spouse or family by feigning a serious malady? The physician has it easy under such circumstances: he can blandly prescribe some harmless pills—and later collect his fee. But what can the minister do? I believe there are cases in which he may be bluntly frank, even at the risk of incurring deep displeasure. Late reports from the medical world indicate that possibly 60 per cent of those who call for the doctor have their own imaginations to thank for what is alleged to be sickness.

What shall the minister do when in a certain case he is morally certain that recovery is unlikely? My sole word of advice is that he be tenderly honest.

What of the invalid who cannot die, but lies days without end, hopeless of recovery? Ah, one can only try. Perhaps it will help to assure the afflicted that God needs those who can suffer patiently as examples of the operation of His grace. But, when the inevitable next question comes, "Why did He choose me to be the one who must illustrate His grace in this painful way?" what can the minister say? There are some perplexities in connection with one's care of the sick which simply baffle. The whole question of unequal human suffering is one which no one's wisdom has been successful in exploring. Of one thing, however, the minister must himself be certain: that God always has His reason for His every decision and act. Let him confess frankly to the inquiring sufferer that he does not know, but that all his experience has convinced him that God's ways are right and wise.

The minister should do all he can for the sick. More is not required of him. He will discover, if he bends heart, mind and will to the effort, that the cases in which he can happily help far outnumber those in which he is completely at a loss.

What of the cases in which physical health has evidently been dissipated by abuse of the physical self? Overwork under the spur of wanting to get rich—indulgence in liquor—sexual indiscretions—malnutrition because of overdone thrift—pure carelessness of exposure—morbid brooding—persistently keeping late hours—carelessness in diet—too much addiction to tobacco—failure to take needed outdoor exercise—there is a long list of avoidable causes that contribute to physical breakdowns. The minister who is a true shepherd of souls will not hesitate, excepting his first call in a given case, to remind the sufferer that we often are the architects of our own misfortunes.

The minister should be scrupulously cautious not to say or to do anything, which may later be turned to his discredit, when he is alone in the sickroom with a person of the opposite sex. There have been quite well substantiated cases in which women have staged a sickness to entice the minister. Enough said.

It should be unnecessary to caution the minister against being more attentive to the sick parishioner who is wealthy than to the one who is poor; but I fear this is necessary. Under usual circumstances moneyed parishioners are so desirable as assets to the average congregation that the minister feels under compulsion to make use of every opportunity to convince such parishioners that they are highly appreciated. What more exploitable opportunity than a case of sickness? More than that, the sickroom in many a poor man's little home is often far from inviting.

Another element in the reckoning is the general proneness of the households in which there is sickness to feel neglected and even to complain publicly although there may not be the slightest reason. Now, it is less hazardous to have a poor church member dissatisfied than it is to have a heavy payer displeased. All in all, the temptations to be partial among the sick of a parish are so many and so strong that I shall not apologize for having cautioned the minister against unwise and unfair discrimination.

Hospital visits, especially those in wards and in semiprivate rooms, cannot fully take on the character of sick visits in the patient's home. But the presence of nurses or other patients should not deter the minister from conducting devotions with his patient. I believe that the young minister is often moved, out of "politeness" to others who would be within reach of his voice, to limit his pastoral service to saying, as he bids the patient farewell, "I hope the good Lord will see you through," or merely, "Well, Brother (Sister), God bless you!" This will not do. A pastor's unafraid ministry to the sick under such circumstances has often been a blessing, an appreciated blessing, to others in the ward who lacked spiritual care.

It is no secret that there have been and still are physicians who dislike to have their patients visited by ministers. In all probability there have been and still are ministers who justly merit the physicians' dislike. There are pastors who carry no sunshine with them, only gloom, when they attend the sick. There are pastors whose prayers are not confiding conversations with a loving Heavenly Father, but depressing ramblings and moralizings. I want no physician (some of whom, I am sorry to say, see in a patient only an ailing animal) to presume to dictate to me in the matter of my shepherding the soul of an ailing parishioner. At the same time, I want to remember, as I minister to the sick, that the gospel of Christ is the power of God unto salvation, and that Christ came into the flesh not to condemn the world but to redeem and to heal.

I take for granted that the understanding minister will realize that, in the case of serious illness, he has an important service to render, not only to the sick but to the family of the sick. Illness is often used in God's providence to open doors, break down resistances and rout indifference in hearts and souls which He has been unable to reach by other means. It is for God's servant to consider this, and wisely to make use of the offered opportunities. But let it be borne in mind that wisdom must dominate. Careless young fellows and thoughtless young women whose fathers or mothers may be at the point of death do not want to be scared into repentance and resolutions by the minister's capitalizing in a crude way on the anxiety in their hearts. Nor do heedless parents relish having the serious illness of a loved child held as a dagger to their hearts by a clumsy minister to exact promises of deeper interest in the Bible and the Church.

When the minister is asked by the family to be present at

an operation, as is sometimes his experience, and then has what he thinks is good reason to doubt correct ethics of the physician or the surgeon, he is indeed in an embarrassing situation. I think that he can only report to the family that he acceded to the request, but that, not being versed in surgery, he can only report that the surgeon seemed to be competent and skillful.

7. WHEN THE MINISTER CALLS ON WOMEN MEMBERS

Calls—calls—calls: they are a specter, let us confess frankly, which is constantly lurking in the background, or brazenly strutting in the foreground, to keep us uneasy. A few ministers, I think, who are by nature blessed (?) with dispositions which incline them to enjoy spending a great deal of their time chatting with friends in public and in these friends' homes, are not in the least disconcerted by the demand that the minister devote a large share of his time to making calls. But most of us, realizing that calls on the sick, the specially tried and afflicted, the bereaved, the stranger, the so-called prospect, are necessary, and being fully willing to use hours each day in making such calls, dread the demand that we spend precious hours week by week in purely social visiting in the homes of our parishioners.

One of the elements of our dread is that pastoral calls must be made in the afternoons. Our five available evenings in the week are mostly taken by meetings and special engagements. Morning social calls are not welcomed in many homes. The afternoon situation in the average home is that no one is there except the lady of the house—the husband being away at his occupation, the children in school.

Calling, then, in very many cases resolves itself into the pastor's "dropping in" and having a chat alone with the lady of the house. This places him in a situation so embarrassing, even dangerous, that he may well devote deep reflection to the question of extremely discreet conduct in this part of his work. Gossip is a disreputable enemy, howbeit a wily and powerful one; and the minister's intended pastoral calls are a productive source of zestful material for the maw of the gossip. The young minister does not yet understand this, and many a maturer man has failed to take it into account. Let me set it down, plain and positive: it is a dangerous practice for any minister to call on a woman alone in her home.

But what can the luckless man do? A number of expedients suggest themselves. For one thing, he can take his congregation into his confidence and frankly and openly tell them what his embarrassment is. This will give gossip and gossips a fairly effective jolt. For another, he can take his wife or, if he is fortunate enough to have one below school age, one of his children with him. Do not laugh. I am serious about the child. Even so young a child is an efficient bodyguard.

Again, these home calls must be very brief. If the minister finds that there are circumstances which require a long call, let him postpone their consideration to a time when other members of the household are at home. Further, let the minister beware of calling frequently on any one woman. It is almost a deathblow to any minister's reputation to have the gossips, male or female, of his community truthfully saying, "The preacher's car is in front of Mrs. John Doe's house two or three times every week." No matter if Mrs. Doe is organist, choir mother, president of the missionary society or the ladies' aid, head of the beginners' department of the Sunday School, or secretary of the nursery roll, the minister has no valid reason for seeing her alone in her home unduly often.

Again, with all due recognition of the desirability of having the minister present at the evening meetings of the various church groups ("Oh, we just can't get along without him, and people just won't attend if he is not there to give a little talk!"), if important pastoral calls are imprudent during the day, a congregation's organizations must be made to understand that these calls take precedence over the usual group meetings, and these meetings must manage without him.

To add to the minister's perplexities, it will have to be said that many a Christian church has in its membership women to whom the questionable epithet, "designing," is fully applicable. Whether from ordinary mischievous playfulness or from a willful desire to get the minister into a predicament, they concoct one scheme after another to get to see him alone. He must early in his ministry learn to be more than a match for such designing females. Sometimes they cannot be squelched unless he becomes positively rude. Very well, let him be rude to them.

There are also those hypochondriac women who demand the minister's frequent calls because they are allegedly sick. They must, of course, be visited in the daytime. They are a real problem; but he must not allow the problem to baffle him. The problem deepens when he asks himself, "How can I offer prayer, asking God to heal this woman, when I know she is not sick?" His best line of action will be to pop in, say a few breezy words, and leave in a moment. He need not fear that he will thus risk his reputation as a good pastor by apparently neglecting such "sick" ones. Their own relatives will be the first to excuse him, for they know.

8. WHEN THE MINISTER FUNCTIONS AS A TEACHER

"Teaching them to observe all things whatsoever I have commanded you." Jesus made his apostles teachers. There is a difference between preaching and teaching. A sermon should never be a classroom lecture, nor should it treat a subject as a teacher would treat it. But the preacher is not a master of his calling if he is not able to teach.

Aside from imparting truth through preaching, the minister is rightly called upon to teach. In almost every parish he takes an active part in the work of the Sunday School, Bible School or Church School, whatever one may prefer as the designation of the meetings which most churches conduct regularly on the Lord's Day in addition to the divine service proper.

And in most parishes the minister is the actual teacher of a class, usually the so-called Bible Class, although every class in the school should be and customarily is a Bible class.

Several of our large communions still conduct classes for the preparation of young people, also adults, for intelligent, mature Christian profession of faith and active church membership. They hold the ancient rite of Confirmation still in high reverence. I believe one of the good indications in church circles is the diminishing interest in, and reliance on, persuading people to profess faith and to unite with a church under the stress of emotional enthusiasm.

When instruction preparatory to public confession and reception into visible church membership is practiced, the minister usually is, and he should be, the teacher. I am old-fashioned enough to think that the acquaintance which the minister makes with children and young people while thus instructing them is an immensely valuable asset.

With this in mind, the minister must learn the principles of successful and effective pedagogy. The school world has been extensively victimized by the faddist, and this cheerful enthusiast has done much to discredit all systematizing and methodizing of the teacher's activity. The fact remains that teaching worthy of the name must be organized. The minister who acquaints himself with the underlying ideas and the effectual routines of imparting instruction is wise.

A lack of painstaking thoroughness often characterizes the teaching efforts of the minister. He is human; the time required and the nervous energy consumed in the exercise of thorough teaching are not readily sacrificed, especially by that large number of busy ministers whose tastes and preferences are for other departments of their many-sided vocation. "There is no royal road to knowledge" is equally true of the learner and the teacher. An amount of drudgery will always attach to teaching, even the imparting of the glorious truths of the gospel. The minister must not consider himself above the sweat and toil of the schoolmaster.

This means that he is rightly expected to devote time, thought and sacrifice, not only to actual instruction but also to careful preparation for the task in general and for each lesson period in particular. Some people have the notion that a minister should be able, at any time and in any place, to rise and give instruction in any lesson. For them to think this is not dangerous; but when the minister himself has this notion, there is real danger. The smart-alecky minister is simply inviting disaster. Real teachers have always been humble men and women, their efforts at mastering subjects having convinced them that "there are more things in heaven and earth, Horatio, than are dreamt of in your philosophy." If you want to get embarrassingly cornered, neglect preparation when you are called upon to teach.

One of the risks of being a teacher is the almost inevitable necessity to discipline. Parents usually, to their own and their children's loss, support their children when teachers discipline them. While the minister cannot apply corporal punishment, he will soon have a demoralized group of children on his hands if he allows misbehavior to pass unnoticed when he teaches a class. Just what course to pursue in individual cases cannot be set down here; but this much can be said: the minister who wins the love and respect of his pupils will, with patience, conquer the misbehaving class member and be able to impose a checking hand when disturbances threaten. He had better give the questions of discipline and control an adequate amount of serious thought and study in advance.

9. WHEN THE MINISTER HAS A WEDDING

To my mind, nothing is more solemn than the rite in which a man and a woman publicly attest that they will be for life husband and wife; and, so attesting and avowing, receive the blessings of the Church. There is so much levity perpetrated by good-hearted, thoughtless, as well as by misanthropic people, in regard to marriage, that I feel that the minister should determinedly refuse to take part in it. When God joins two people together as they are joined in marriage, God's servant in the Ministry may well lift the marriage ceremony to the loftiest heights.

With his exalted estimate of the marriage estate he may also well combine an appreciation of the bride's solicitudes. She wants the service just so. Perhaps she is including more "style" than is appropriate; but, after all, that will do no harm. I consider it in perfect consonance with my ministerial dignity to rehearse, according to the bride's wishes and directions, the marriage service, whether in the home or in the church. When she defers to the minister's judgment and experience and asks him about various little details, it is not fitting for him, in a pooh-pooh vein, to tell her that anything will do, and this and that does not matter. Take her seriously and be serious. The Saviour of the world had a heart for young couples. He not only attended the wedding at Cana, but he saved the bride and the groom from a very painful predicament.

One of my crotchets is to perform the marriage ceremony without any book in my hands. I do not like to read, "The Rev. Mr. John Doe *read* the marriage service." Reading something from a book is not so impressive as saying it from heart to heart; and pretending to create the effect by glancing from the book occasionally to meet the couple's eyes is not convincing. Also, with a book in his hand, the minister cannot so safely and so gracefully perform the ring service. With a book in one hand he cannot impose both hands on the heads of the kneeling couple as he pronounces the prayer of blessing on bride and groom. Memorize the service. Most ministers (not all). can repeat the Lord's Prayer, the Apostles' Creed, and the Aaronic benediction without a book in hand. The marriage service can be so spoken.

After the service comes the reception, usually also a wedding feast. Of course, the minister is invited and, of course, he accepts the invitation. What of his deportment for the occasion? He will find himself in the midst of jesters and jokers; and wedding jokers have an inclination to employ jokes which are suggestive. He will find himself among people who intend to play pranks at the expense of the bride and groom. He may even be approached to enlist as a helper in what are so tragically and mistakenly called practical jokes.

Preacher, while you have no call to be a kill-joy when people are making merry at a happy wedding feast, neither have you a call to be the "life of the party." Do not forget that the feast is in connection with a step so solemn that its importance for the newly wedded pair cannot be overestimated. Your role at a wedding feast is not an easy one. Act it sympathetically, understandingly and convincingly.

Do you know that with all the light-hearted merry-making a wedding still—yes, even in these changed times—brings heaviness and misgivings into the hearts of the parents of both bride and groom? Mother seldom feels entirely carefree when her boy becomes one with some girl, or when her girl places all her life into the hands of some boy. Father, not so demonstrative as Mother, has his feelings, too. What will his life now be, when the daughter who always was there to show him filial love has gone away with "another man"? He and his boy have always consulted each other. It will be different now.

Mr. Minister, there is something infinitely fine for you to do for this mother and this father. You will not accomplish it if your hand is bungling as it will be if your heart has not busied itself to learn all the ins and outs of human nature. One of the distinguishing marks of that Good Shepherd whose undershepherd you are is expressed in these words: "He had compassion." Do not wait for bereavements and funerals to have compassion. Weddings should call it into precious service.

Performing the ceremony with which man and woman begin their married life establishes a relation between their pastor and them which is peculiar, and which can be inestimably precious (except, of course, in drop-in marriages of people whom the minister does not personally know and may never see again). One of the surprises of my ministerial experience has been to discover again and again that people whom I have married continue to hold me in a strange remembrance on that account; yes, to go so far as to give me credit for having so indissolubly and happily united them. I am convinced that a tender relation can be created between him and the couple when the minister, conducting himself decorously, becomes the instrument of solemnizing their marriage. The minister becomes in an unusual degree and an extraordinary sense their pastor; and this means, if children are given to them, the pastor of their family.

It would be a dull and uncomprehending minister, indeed, who could not see in this providence an opportunity for exercising unhindered the gracious office of shepherd of the family's souls. They will need shepherding, no matter how much sunshine brightens their lives. Clouds will gather, storms will break; and, somehow, it is natural for a wedded couple, when a tempest strikes, to think of the pastor who married them as being in the ship with them. Maybe, although he does not have the authority of Him who said to the Sea of Galilee, "Peace! Be still!" and brought upon its turbulent waters a great calm—maybe, after all, he can be so trustworthy and spirit-filled that their ship will ride through the waves into smooth waters again.

10. When the Minister Has an Assistant Minister

In the business world I have heard it said that partnerships are hazardous arrangements. Partners in business are reported to have all sorts of frictions and tensions. Sometimes, where they agree fairly well, their wives have jealousies and grievances which arise because their husbands are really or supposedly suffering unfair treatment at the hands of the other partners.

Ordination for the Holy Ministry does not change men's nature. It seems difficult for two pastors to work together in one and the same parish without friction. In those church

groups in which vicarships are general the student in the
seminary, knowing that he will likely for his first years in the
Ministry be a vicar, gets a certain *habitus* which makes
strained relations between pastor and assistant less probable.
But in most of our church bodies this is not usual.

Whose fault is it when tensions of this kind are generated?
Sometimes the pastor's, sometimes the vicar's, sometimes (and
very often) the church members'. It is inevitable that any
pastor will, in the course of a pastorate in any parish, take
lines of action and express opinions and judgments which are
not acceptable to every member of his flock. The disagreements may be such as to cause resentment to arise against the
minister. It continues, smolders, and finally, when conditions
are just so, it bursts into flame. The vicar provides the means
for making the flame effective. Human nature suggests to the
aggrieved church member to play up to the assistant pastor,
praising his sermons without saying one good word for the
pastor's, inviting him to family social functions, taking him to
the ball game, giving him generous presents, and all the while
making the procedure ostentatious and gradually winning
other members' preference for the assistant. Absalom stole the
hearts of Israel away from David. The hearts of many church
members have been stolen away from the pastor and laid at
the assistant's feet.

What can the minister do about it? I have never been surprised that one minister after another in our connection has,
even when pressed by well-meaning church members and
officers, declined to have a vicar engaged. I have heard fine
strong men in the Ministry say that they would carry the load
alone as long as they could, then either retire or ask for a
transfer to a parish in which the load would be lighter. In
most cases I admired their foresight.

Incidentally, the question, whether any parish should be
allowed to grow so numerically large that it overtaxes a minister who has average strength and ability, is not a foolish one.
Large parishes make for impressiveness as to the Kingdom's

greatness, but they do not make for real efficiency in organization, nor for that individual pastoral attention which so many souls require.

Assuming, though, that a minister is serving a parish in which an assistant minister is indispensable, what can he do to keep all moving smoothly? For one thing, he can earnestly cultivate those graces and that disposition which will make tensions less likely and which will, if they develop, keep him master of the situation. Let him be considerate, wise, prudent, patient, and possessed of a bountiful supply of sweet reasonableness. Let him beware of taking himself for granted. Let him realize that in some respects his assistant excels him; and that, fresh from seminary, he has possibly acquired some techniques which formerly were not in the course. Rather than try to eclipse the younger man, let him give him free opportunities. Let him accustom himself to thinking, "He must increase, but I must decrease." Doing all this, he will find himself increasing and will discover that his parishioners appreciate his fairness and magnanimity. Will this be playing with fire? I think not; anyhow it need not be.

Let us give a little more attention to the supposedly well-entrenched minister's aptitude to take too many things in regard to himself for granted. He will always have some "loyal" church members who will adhere to him without questioning; but at the same time there will be many more who demand constant "delivery of the real goods." Also, there may be those who are plain "nasty" enough to want to undermine him. The obvious safeguard is for the minister, no matter how high his ability, to keep himself constantly critical of his own performance and production—honestly and pitilessly critical.

When the minister favors his assistant in various ways, he must beware of doing it patronizingly. If an assistant pastor is worth having at all, he has spirit and excusable pride. He is deserving of respect, also of the genuine respect of the pastor *primarius*. Even assuming a paternal interest in the younger man needs safeguarding, lest it become an indulgent condescension. Advice should always be given in the form of suggestion. Merited praise should be bestowed with genuine warmth. Many a minister's difficulties with his curate are of his own making, and steady skill and wise planning are the price he must pay if all is to proceed happily. A good motto is, "Put yourself in his place."

11. WHEN THE MINISTER IS AN ASSISTANT MINISTER

Playing second fiddle would be more agreeable if there were no first fiddler. Serving as assistant pastor is, in a sense, playing second fiddle. When two fiddles are played well, as first and second, the music is charming. But when the second fiddler forgets or misunderstands his role, the effect is not only disharmony but often disastrous jangling.

The man who plays second fiddle ably deserves plenty of credit. If the music is harmonious, let him console himself by remembering that, whereas there is more glory for the player of the lead part, he after all deserves and receives the esteem of those who understand harmony. The orchestra director values every instrument and every player. You recall that Paul said he cared little for the approval of men, just so the Master knew and approved.

I think that the main trouble in the life of the assistant pastor is that, instead of trying to make himself a first-class assistant, he is constantly itching to invade the preserves of the head pastor. To change the figure—he is not inclined to stay in his stall. He should have settled in his mind, before accepting a position as assistant, that he would be content with a minor (?) role for a few years. If he would only reflect that his freedom from the chief responsibilities and his opportunity, by quiet observation, to absorb valuable experience more than offset the unwelcome features of his status.

One of his chief efforts must, in the nature of the case, be to deal circumspectly with the ingratiating church members who are bent on annoying the pastor by promoting the interests of the assistant. Much as we (the usual run of us, ordained or unordained) enjoy flattery, the assistant minister must steel himself against the insidious menace. He need not be uncharitably suspicious, but he has every reason to be on his guard most alertly against both the designing church member and his own weak nature.

There should be a clear understanding, preferably in writing and signed, on the part of both pastor and assistant before the latter accepts his position as such, of the duties and the sphere of action which are to be his; and then a meticulously conscientious hewing to the line. Let the assistant bear in mind that he and the pastor are being closely watched for frictions which may so easily develop. Let him cultivate an open frankness with the pastor. Let him refrain from making any decisions, promises and arrangements which are not his to make independently. Let him solemnly vow that he will excel as an assistant and as nothing else. It may be that he has a better theological and practical training than his superior; that he has the more likable personality; that he is a more interesting preacher; that he is a more congenial "mixer": all this does not make him either head pastor or competitor.

Chapter 3

THE MINISTER'S HOME LIFE

1. WHEN THE MINISTER REMAINS A BACHELOR

The young man who has just entered the Ministry and has not yet taken unto himself "a helpmeet for him" may skip this chapter—unless he is hopelessly committed to celibacy. The minister under consideration here is the honest-to-goodness bachelor.

Let me say in all sincerity and sympathy that, although I have been well acquainted with his kind in the persons of various individuals, I am at a loss in regard to him. As an honest preacher of God's Word and God's ways, he must repeatedly extol the beautiful tenderness of the marital relation and of home life. How can he do this unembarrassed when he, by eschewing the one, makes the other impossible for himself?

I know it is possible for a dietitian to advise the eating of certain foods, but to refrain from partaking of them himself, saying, "Somehow, they do not agree with me." It is possible for a physician to compose a diet list for a patient, and, when the patient rebels and says, "Doctor, I just can't eat one-half of those unpalatable items; and I happen to know that you yourself despise them, for I have heard your wife say that there is no use to cook them for you," to answer, "Yes, but I am allergic to those." Such evasions, however, do not deeply impress the listener. Even if they did, the position of the bachelor minister would not thereby be made more tenable.

So—what shall I say when the minister is a confirmed bachelor? How and where shall he live? Shall he occupy a few rooms in the parsonage, the rest to be left bare and unoccupied? Shall a small apartment be rented for him and the parsonage be rented to others? Shall he "keep bachelor's hall," which means doing his own housework and preparing at least some of his meals? Will it be safe for him to hire a woman as housekeeper, and live under the same roof with her? Can he rely upon his absolute purity of purpose to shield him and her from the stabs of gossiping tongues?

There is no satisfactory solution. The housekeeper arrangement is far too much of a risk. She would have to be so old to make it safe to have her, that she would be unable to do much housework. Engaging rooms in a private home makes it quite difficult for distressed members to visit the minister to unburden themselves of troubles. Besides, it usually leaves the minister alone with the lady of the house—rich food for gossips. Occupying rooms in a men's apartment house bars women members from seeing the pastor alone. Occupying a few rooms in the parsonage and keeping bachelor's hall there presents the same objection.

When the pastor has aged parents, or a widowed mother, or a maiden sister who can keep house for him, there is a quite happy escape from these embarrassments.

The advisability of an arrangement whereby the pastor, bachelor or married, has his office hours at the church is questionable. Designing women are not afraid to try to ply their artifices on a minister even within consecrated precincts. To be in the office alone with a young woman secretary or church clerk, or with a deaconess, is to invite not only harassing rumors but dangerous temptations. "Beware the woman!" may well be posted in large type in the daily memorandum of every minister, especially the bachelor. But the bachelor must be careful likewise lest he be accused of too friendly companionship with little girls, and with boys. I have known the damaging tongue of scandal to spit on ministers' reputations so often that I feel I am not needlessly alarmed in this regard.

Another considerable danger which stalks the bachelor minister is the development of oddities and eccentricities in his makeup. He is peculiarly liable to becoming what is very picturesquely and pointedly called a "screwball." Living an abnormal life is not conducive to remaining well balanced. And it does not help any minister to acquire the name of being "queer."

Another weakness of the bachelor minister is his inability to give needed advice in matters that have to do with sexual relations, with the rearing of children, and with the smoothing of the rough places which sometimes form in wedlock. Mothers and wives with delicate questions to settle will not accost the bachelor minister with great confidence. Young people about to venture into matrimony will hardly seek his counsel; and it is becoming more and more generally admitted that premarital advice by the pastor is a prime desideratum.

To sum it up: when the minister is a bachelor he is in a precarious state and lacks proficiencies which are almost essential in the Ministry.

2. When the Minister Chooses a Life Companion

When a church selects a minister and in its investigation as to his desirability includes inquiries about his wife, it has sometimes been remarked that such inquiries are positively out of order. The church is calling a minister, not his wife. It pays him a salary, his wife not a penny. It assigns duties to him in its call, not to her.

People who utter such opinions are paying a poor compliment both to womanhood in general and to their own intelligence. Without intending to hand womankind the usual blandishments and flatteries, I want simply to call attention to the amazing influence which both womankind and individual women invariably exercise. Bear in mind that, when we call "man" the climax of God's creative activity in the universe, the word means "mankind," and it imperatively includes woman. Furthermore, if God's creation was progressive throughout, woman, being created last, would necessarily have to be classed as the ultimate climax and man would have to take lower rank.

The pastor's wife, uncalled and unsalaried, has a leading role to act in the shepherding of any congregation: a role which includes its men, its women, its youth, its boys, its girls, its babies—and its pastor. How much of this does the average theological student have in mind when he makes his decision as to the girl he will ask to marry him?

This question leads us to other, more difficult ones: Should any man choose a life companion on the basis of mental calculation in regard to her fitness to be a help in the work he has chosen for life? Is marriage a matter of personal love, or is it a matter of business partnership, to state it crudely? Should a man's heart, or his head, decide whom he would like to marry? Is love an emotion, a passion, instinctively yearning for a correspondent, or is it a well-regulated, calmly controlled innate inclination which must above all else listen to reason?

What questions with which to grapple! Yet they stare us in the face and we dare not try to evade them. In facing them, let us not be intimidated regarding that almost universally accepted assumption that love should be the basis of marriage, and that marriage cannot possibly be a blessing unless love has led to it. As Scripture has it, "The heart is deceitful"; and it is very deceitful in young people. What they may think and feel to be that precious love on which a happy marriage and a blessed life can be founded is in thousands of cases a passion which, genuine at the time, may utterly lack the enduring elements which true love must possess.

Someone should write a gripping tract or pamphlet on this subject, and it should be placed immediately into the hands of every man entering theological seminary; and, somehow, he should be made to read it. This tract should not discourage his proper association with the opposite sex, nor should it laugh at him when he thinks he is in love. It should persuade him to lay a hand of restraint on what seems to him to be love. If he is in godly earnestness about making the Ministry his lifework, surely he can make the sacrifice of not committing himself so far, either in declarations by words or in attentions paid, that a maiden has an indisputable right to expect a proposal from him. Putting his own love on probation, as it were, will work no particular hardship. At any rate, his seminary tasks should not and will not, if conscientiously pursued, leave him much time for assiduous love-making.

Now let him, without our in the least doubting the sincerity of this thing called love, calmly try to visualize himself and the maiden in question in the pastorate of a given church. Let him seek the advice of those whom he can trust, and from their own experience and honesty of judgment learn what sort of wife will help and what sort of wife will hinder a man in the Ministry.

What, now, if he discovers that the maiden would in all likelihood not make a desirable wife, but finds he loves her so truly that he cannot abide the thought of leaving her? I say without hesitation, then let him "cleave to his [intended] wife" and abandon the Ministry. After all, marriage was instituted before the Ministry. There have been warm arguments, whether the professional Ministry was directly instituted by God, or is an ecclesiastical institution, established by the Church under indirect guidance of the Holy Spirit. Be the correct answer whatever it may, man came first, before the Ministry. Also, the professional Ministry is not the only agency through which Christ's gospel can be heralded. A happily mated layman may accomplish more for the Kingdom than an ill-mated clergyman.

Assuming, now, that a young man, Ministry-bent, is subjecting the question of a minister's wife to serious consideration, what are the qualifications his wife should possess? Do not call me unfeeling because of the number I set down here. It is not my personal judgment but a wide experience that speaks. She should, I hope we may take for granted, be a sincere Christian. She should have a serious, modest and sunny disposition; a school education which was continued at least through high school; an inclination to read solid matter; an ability to "hold her peace"; a love for children, and wanting her own; and a gift for teaching. I might add also: a passion for tidy coiffure and attire, and for tidy housekeeping; sympathy and understanding kindness; serenity and poise; a detestation of slang, of loudness, of chewing gum, and of other evidences of vulgarity; an intense interest in the minister's work; etc.

Might it not be better, if these reflections are correct, for men in the Ministry to remain unmarried? This is for each man himself to decide. A very successful minister, known to all the Church, remained unmarried to the end of his days. He was Paul, the "greatest" of the Apostles. There have been other successful bachelor ministers. But the general opinion of Protestant ministers is that it is far better to marry, as is proved by the fact that almost all of them are married. It is further proved that Protestant churches concur in this opinion, because they shy away when bachelor preachers are recommended for them to call. "It is not good that the man should be alone" is not misinterpreted when it is said to mean, "It is not natural for a man to remain unmarried." Somehow, we married men think something vital and essential is lacking in the man who is not inclined to marry.

This does not mean that any minister should marry against his own inclinations. If he does not have that in his makeup which makes him yearn for a companion in marriage, let him continue his limited functioning as best he can. Those who almost compel an unmarried minister to go afield and yoke himself together with a woman in matrimony are running a desperately serious risk. Let the unmarried minister alone!

3. WHEN THE MINISTER DEALS WITH THE HOME QUESTION

If the deterioration and disintegration of the home has a heavy bearing on the condition of the State, it has an equally alarming bearing on the life of the Church. There are few subjects with which the minister has to deal which are of greater importance than the subject of ordinary day-by-day life in the home—the humblest poverty-plagued home as well as the pretentious mansion. Family life is still fundamental, with all the changes and upheavals which have befallen the time-honored institutions of humanity.

It is difficult for me to see how the minister can successfully meet the many problems which the home presents today unless he himself has a home. For this reason among others, as said before, I favor marriage for the minister. Far be it from me to advocate his seeking a wife as his life companion merely because he needs one to enable him to be professionally efficient. Whether marriages are made in heaven or not may be open to serious debate in view of the numberless unwise unions; but that they should be made in heaven is my honest conviction. The minister should not be expected to contract a marriage of convenience.

It devolves upon the married minister to be an exemplary husband and father. This means not only that he should have the fear of God rule in his household. It means that he should grace himself as a husband with the beautiful conduct which tender love for his wife can alone produce. It means that in his attitude toward his children he should be far different from a hard taskmaster, or an inflexible commandant, or a stupid misinterpreter of the child life and child interest of the times. Parenthood today is not a simple responsibility; but the minister, as a man of God, can meet it if he is selfless enough and thoughtful enough. If we cannot count on him to be both, woe betide us!

Assuming, now, that the minister has a home and a family in it, and that in his home he is acting his role acceptably, a considerable share of his time may well be devoted to the elevation of true Christian home life among his parishioners. Premarital counseling has received much discussion in recent times. The minister may fear that young people, about to be married, have their heads so full of plans for the event itself and for the material setting of their married life, that they will give little worth-while attention to what he may safely say about the serious elements of wedlock. Nevertheless, the opinion prevails that he may do much lasting good by counseling young people before they take the step which should mean that they will love, honor and keep each other until death may part them, and that they will keep themselves only unto each other.

In this counseling, religion should, of course, be made prominent. Are the contracting parties of one and the same faith? Is one of them churchless, and probably atheistic? Perhaps they have given no thought to the many strains thrown on the marriage tie by a difference in this regard. Have they considered the begetting and rearing of children? Have they given thought to finance? Have they the approval of their parents for the marriage? Does each have a different circle of friends? Have they considered adjusting their likes and dislikes? The field of discussion is wide. Some ministers spend several hours in premarital counseling with each couple applying.

The minister's somewhat frequent visits to the homes of newly-weds, made at times when they are both at home, will mean much. "A stitch in time saves nine." He should know that marital disagreements usually arise over matters which in themselves are mere trifles. Helping young married people to avoid a first dissension is important.

Too many homes do not have an altar. What can the minister to do to persuade married people, whether they have children or not, to practice daily united devotions? Sometimes he will have to illustrate this beautiful rite by giving the family an actual demonstration. His repeated inquiries, whether such devotions are regularly practiced, will help greatly toward the desired goal.

Rearing children has become largely a matter of providing physical necessities and luxuries, and, for the rest, letting the child do as it pleases and spend its time where it chooses. Old-fashioned as the idea of discipline is, the minister has a call to advocate it ceaselessly. Juvenile delinquency rarely follows careful training. It is not as a rule acceptable to advise careless or doting fathers and mothers in the matter of more rigid discipline for the child. The minister must take the risk.

Whether or not he has a high regard for psychology and psychiatry, it is for the minister to apply much thought to the mental and spiritual processes which go forward in two people who are living in wedlock. Even in what are called well-regulated unions all sorts of tensions develop. In hundreds of cases a tactfully managed conversation will ease a tension and prevent a snapping of nerves. The minister is often the friend for whom such conversation is a responsibility. And when a rift does occur between husband and wife, the minister dare not throw up his hands in dismay and conclude that all is lost. There are thousands of couples living happily together in marriage who occasionally have had very serious disagreements. There are other thousands living apart, either legally divorced or simply separated, because no one attempted to effect a reconciliation when a quarrel arose. I think experience shows that a minister's interposition in "family quarrels" is less likely to be resented than that of any other friend.

4. WHEN THE MINISTER HAS MARITAL DIFFICULTIES

No apology is here offered for my position that in such case I expect more of the minister than of his wife. I have known some ministers' wives who deserved sound spankings for their indiscretions, their folly, their willfulness. Just the same, the woman is of the "frailer" sex; and, despite the mannish airs many women today affect, they are still, fortunately, characterized by their sex. This, I have always held, is not in any degree a disgrace or a weakness. Let every woman be womanly. But, when she is, let the man to whom she is married always bear in mind, not that he belongs to a higher order of creatures, but that constitutionally he is less sensitive and should be abler to endure jolts and knocks.

There is no conceivable method by which to insure a happy choice of wife to the young man minded to enter the Ministry. It would be folly to try to fly in the face of nature and say that the young man's heart should step in the background, and that his head, enlightened by considerations of proved importance and value, should decide what woman he should ask to be his life partner. True love should be the impulse of his wooing, not calm dispassionate calculation. But—and this is important enough to repeat—imagined true love is sometimes not actually love. For this reason the young man with the Ministry in view should again and again be cautioned not to be hasty in love-making. It is not an exaggeration to say that in the Ministry oftener than in any other vocation a wife can make or break her husband.

One of the frequent sources of difficulty between husband and wife in the Ministry is the assumption and maintenance of an air of superiority on the man's part because of his erudition. Even though his wife be a college graduate, she has not studied Hebrew, and in all probability has not gone deeply into Greek, if at all; nor has she acquainted herself with the abstruseness of theological philosophies. It seems that it is as natural for some ministers on this account to parade themselves to their wives' torture as it is for a boy to put on high and mighty airs because he has found a bird's nest which the other fellows have not discovered. Such annoyance on the minister's part is proof that, for one thing, he is not truly erudite; and, for another, that he has failed to acquire the fine sense of consideration for others' feelings without which a person cannot be a truly Christlike servant of the Master.

So much for the day-by-day, year-in-and-year-out life of the minister and his wife. But what if marital tragedy actually stalks into the parsonage? With all the minister's sympathetic consideration for his wife, she may be "impossible." Perhaps she had not intelligently counted the cost of being a lady of the manse. Perhaps she is unwilling to make the sacrifices required by her husband's position. Perhaps she is unregenerate enough to indulge in flirtations and serious indiscretions with other men. Then—what to do?

I believe that the minister need only make sure that he himself is blameless in connection with her lapse in order to insure for himself a fair verdict and considerate treatment by his parish and his community. It is a terrible experience to have such calamity befall the minister; but he need not conclude that it disqualifies him for further service in the Holy Ministry.

It may be that tragedy enters the parsonage in form not quite so hideous, yet hurtful enough. The minister's wife may be a gossip, a scold, a mischief-maker, a gadabout, worldly minded and worldly acting. It is little consolation to him to be told that he should have studied her character and inclinations before he engaged himself to marry her. Little comfort can be extended to him now. Sometimes it may alleviate the harm to have some congregational or synodical officer counsel with him and her together. A woman must be exceptionally obtuse and obstinate not to yield when it is made plain to her that her ways are endangering her husband's position and her own maintenance.

There have been some cases in which the minister's wife has so completely forgotten her marriage vows that she has refused to accompany her husband to a certain parish where he has been called, or refused to interest herself at all in the work he had to do. God pity him. This is about all that can be said in such a case.

Throughout this discussion let it be borne in mind that the minister himself must constantly be on guard lest he be to blame. One of his most difficult activities, strange as this may sound, is to be a good minister and at the same time a good husband.

5.   WHEN THE MINISTER HAS CHILDREN

He should have them. A home is not really complete without them. If, as is sometimes the case, there can be none, the minister and his wife may very properly give serious consideration to the adoption of children. The presence and the rearing of children in a home bring so much that is desirable into the home that there is no question in my mind as to their desirability.

The pulpit does not say much in our times about the responsibility of married people to have children. In this regard the pulpit is neglecting to reflect not only the evident will of God but also the cry of economic and material welfare. Childless nations do not prosper. Childless marriage is not normal. More stress is being laid by unbelieving national leaders on the propagation of nations than by supposedly intelligent and conscientious churchmen.

But producing children does not complete the married minister's duty. These children must be reared, and reared properly. The fact that a child is born to the parsonage does not mean that it will just naturally grow up a perfect boy or girl in the atmosphere of the parsonage. Indeed, it is for certain reasons exceptionally difficult to rear the preacher's boys and girls.

One of these reasons is that many foolish church members insist on spoiling them. The minister's children are petted and pampered, not only by silly spinsters and other women, but by the men of the parish. Entirely too much attention is accorded to them. Few children can remain unspoiled under such conditions.

Another reason is that other people's children on the playground, in school, everywhere, expect better conduct of the minister's children than of their other mates, and, often in irritatingly mocking manner, make it plain that they do. It takes a lot of moral stamina in a boy to keep him straight when some other boy jeers, "Of course you don't dare, because you're the preacher's boy!" Do you wonder that, thus stung, the preacher's boy plunges into evil-doing?

What can the minister do about rearing his children properly under the generally prevailing circumstances? One thing is certain: he has no right to withdraw into his sanctum (Is it really that?) and turn the training of his offspring over to his wife. Hand in hand, and with perfect understanding and harmony, let them make themselves loved and respected by their children. Bearing in mind what dire consequences come when the minister's children do go astray, let them firmly, intelligently and lovingly address themselves to the task of rearing children who will be a joy to their hearts and an honor to the parsonage. It can be done, and it has been done in thousands of cases. The parsonage has no reason to blush on account of the children it has produced. Its black sheep have been surprisingly few.

The minister's ingenuity is taxed to the utmost by those members of his parish who think, or pretend to think, that his children should be deprived of the various advantages and accessories which most other children nowadays enjoy. I am speaking of church members who insist that the preacher's children should be dressed primly, avoiding the fancies of current styles: the girls must have no money spent on their hair-do; the boys do not need skates and baseball gloves and tennis rackets. Going to any theater is strictly taboo. Soda-fountain treats must be few and far between. Music lessons—well, well! fifty cents a lesson is enough. Vacation trips—dancing—card-playing? There are in these advanced times still plenty of people who think the minister should not have money to spend on such nonsense, much of which they call downright sin; and there are others who think that in these respects the minister's children should be totally abnormal, not even caring for them.

Let the minister be positive and fearlessly make it clear that his children are not to have their young lives made bleak and unnatural by his compliance with absurd ideas which are at home in "batty" heads. His children are in the same world with other people's children. They have legitimate cravings for fun and for material enjoyments. When it comes to the question whether to satisfy prudish people by making one's own children needlessly unhappy, there should be only one plausible answer. The minister's children have rights. Let their father defend these rights. Since when, anyhow, is there a double moral standard?

But, on the other hand, the minister must be careful not to join the increasing number of brainless parents who allow their children to run things as they choose. In a day when certain philosophies insist that there is no evil in children—only "nature"; that every child must be left perfectly free to express itself in word and act; that the child's will (willfulness) must never be suppressed: the parsonage parent has an opportunity to shine, and the opportunity should not be missed. Juvenile delinquency, a beast which has us terrified so that we stand aghast and desperate, can be traced to its lair. This beast comes forth out of the foolishly fond hearts of indulgent (or indolent) fathers and mothers who fail to make their homes truly Christian.

But here again the minister's task is harder than that of the average parent. He is in danger of making the religion in his home religiosity, of losing sight of the fact that God gave us bodies as well as souls. Austerity may take the place of firmness: legalism may supplant the evangelical spirit.

The minister's hardest test comes when his sons are leaving boyhood for young manhood, when his daughters are subtly emerging into young womanhood. It is then, however, that wise training in their childhood bears delectable fruit. It is

still true that "just as the twig is bent, the tree's inclin'd."
The properly trained minister's children will themselves become guardians of virtue and uprightness for others.

Must the minister's son, to fulfill his rightful destiny, follow
him into the Ministry? Must his daughter become a deaconess,
a foreign missionary, or a preacher's wife? Emphatically—no!
It is gratifying to the minister, to be sure, to see his son select
the Ministry as his life calling; and he is in position to send
him into this calling with distinct advantages. On the other
hand, it is not contributory to virility and variety in the Ministry to have it become, as it were, an heirloom, handed down
from father to son in unbroken succession. We want new
blood in the Ministry regularly; and we want this blood to
carry into the Ministry the elements of various backgrounds—
to come from the farm, the shop and the mill; from the
metropolis and the village; from the rich man's mansion and
the poor widow's cottage. The minister need not feel bound,
either by a desire to strengthen the Ministry or a compelling
sense of duty, to exert special pressure on his children in order
to lead them into the professional service of the Church.

Besides, ministers' sons and daughters have, by hundreds
and thousands, made such commendable records in all sorts
of honest vocations as to give the Christian parsonage a high
rating as the source of manifold blessings for humanity. The
question is raised whether they have not exercised greater
beneficent influence than would have been the case had they
chosen vocations closely connected with the Church.

6. WHEN THE MINISTER HAS A YARD TO TEND

How any man can continue in the Ministry without a loving appreciation of lawns and shrubs and trees and flowers is
one of the mysteries I have been unable to pierce. I think I
have met only a very few who lacked this appreciation.
But—to appreciate growing things and to do something about
their care are, again, two different things. Give me the minis-

ter who makes sacrifices of either energy or money in order
to surround himself with them.

The parsonage lawns should be equal to the best in the
neighborhood. The parsonage grounds should rank high.
Whether they get their care from the minister's own hands or
not is immaterial; but loving and intelligent care they should
have. Not everybody has a green thumb. But it does not require prize-taking gardening skill to make the yard, large or
small, about the parsonage an attractive one.

Many a minister has, in the act of encouraging things to
grow, found himself growing—growing into a better pastor
and a better preacher. When God said, "Let the earth bring
forth," He was caring for man in various ways. So, give me
the minister who wants the earth about his church and parsonage to bring forth, and who is willing to help it along.

The minister's yard may very properly have a wren house,
a bird bath, or two or three, a pool for fish, a gazing globe, a
sun dial, and, in winter, a bird-feeding station. The parsonage
should be nicely located on a lot not too small, and I mean
every word of this. If churches would only believe it—the
minister's home surroundings have a marked influence on his
service in many ways. Coop a minister up, force him into
tight quarters, and you are well on the way to dwarfing him
mentally and socially. If you want him to grow, normally and
humanly, put him into a setting of growing things. A few
excursions in spring and summer into the rural districts are
not adequate. Give the minister permanent garden surroundings; but, when he has them, let him show appreciation by
caring for them. And here is a concluding whisper: I do not
like to see the minister's wife laboriously pushing a lawn
mower.

Chapter 4

THE MINISTER'S PERSONAL AFFAIRS

1. WHEN THE MINISTER BUYS CLOTHES FOR HIMSELF

The controversy, whether or not the minister should wear "clericals," is still in progress. In some denominations they are the rule; in others, an exception. They offer some advantages. They enable the minister to be known at a glance. This has its advantages and its disadvantages. In some cities it is easier to get by with a traffic law violation when the officer sees that the violator is a "priest." I have been told that it is quite comforting, when one has violated and finds the stern arm of the law stretching out, to see the officer break into a smile and to hear him say, "Oh, excuse me—that's all right, Father!"

I have also been told that the minister, careless of the time, gets readier admittance out of visiting hours in hospitals when he is attired in clericals; but in many years of ministering experience, some of which included visiting in four or five hospitals in one city regularly, my right to enter at any hour was never questioned, and I never wore anything but regulation business clothing. Whenever a new attendant looked doubtful, the mere announcement that I was a clergyman sufficed.

There is also the contention that clericals keep laundry bills lower. Some preachers facetiously refer to clericals as "dirty-shirt outfits."

One of the disadvantages often named is that, when men see at a glance that a man is a minister, they assume an unnatural attitude, making it difficult for the minister to approach them and deal with them as a man's man. Not only do men at once get on their guard, but they often classify the minister as a "sis" or as a highbrow when, as they conceive it, ordinary men's clothes are not good enough for him. On the other hand, there are those who argue that the minister's very attire should be a constant reminder to him that he is not really just another man among men, but is a man of God among men of the world. So the controversy continues.

While it proceeds, it is right, meet and salutary to devote attention to the clothing of the minister who does not affect clericals. He probably feels he has a right to resent being subjected to regulation in this regard; but there are many of his group who most certainly need some kindly direction, and it is here offered.

Let the minister wear what he chooses as long as it does not violate conservative aesthetic taste, or as long as it is not one of the freak styles adopted momentarily by those who want to be so different in attire that the difference startles. He has a full right to wear blue, brown or gray, striped, plaid or tweed suits. Why not? He has a full right to wear single- or double-breasted coats, sack or frock coats. Why not? But, if he has any reason to doubt his own taste in making a wise selection, let him seek and follow good advice. Honestly, usually his wife is competent to give this advice. Let him be sensible and not sensitive about letting her have a hand in his clothing selections.

Shoes, hosiery, shirts, neckwear and hats should all be chosen with care and discrimination. If the minister does wear colored shirts, let the colors be such as will not offend the refined eye. He may wear tan shoes instead of black (but not in the Sunday services). White shoes in summer do not rob him of any worth-while dignity. As for neckties, I shall have to admit that in their selection a man's judgment is truer than a woman's.

A pretty fair guide in getting what is suitable is price.

Cheap articles of attire are not cheap except in appearance. One good article of wear will outlast and "outlook" two poor ones; and good things always cost, but not double. God was most exacting as to the dress of His ministers in the Old Testament. Their attire was rich and expensive. We need not fear His displeasure when we spend good money on our ministerial garb. As for the displeasure of small-minded church members, ignore it. The Ministry is a high calling. Be dressed for your part.

Even when you are spading your garden or mowing your lawn, have a care not to make a scarecrow of yourself. Church members for the most part do not want their minister under any circumstance to look too "common." You can never foresee when some stranger may call; and first impressions are often not erasable. The minister who jumps into his car and runs down town to get a forgotten loaf of bread, wearing the slouch outfit he utilizes when he does garden or cellar work at home, may mortify a church member who happens to be down town with company. The few minutes needed for always looking "decent" are well invested. Good clothes do not keep their good appearance without attention. Suits need cleaning and pressing, hats need sprucing, shoes need polishing, linen needs frequent changing and laundering. The slovenly minister makes sad and serious mistakes, letting his appearance "run down."

Many ministers even in nonliturgical churches now wear the gown in their Sunday services. This is a move in the right direction. That gown not only lifts the minister's administration of the holy service to higher levels; it also covers a multitude of things that had better be covered: awkwardness and ungainliness in physical build, unkemptness in dress, in rural churches often soil and splash on the preacher's clothes. But the wearing of a gown is not in itself sufficient. The gown must be rich and well fitting. The preacher who robes himself in a cheap, slimsy, baggy gown that makes him look like a crooked post with a black rag draped over it should not imagine he is honoring God by decorously attiring himself for service in His house. A frequent remissness in wearing a robe is in using one not long enough to cover one's trousers down to the shoetops. To see shins encased in light-colored trousers sticking out under a black robe is mirth-provoking.

When the minister does not wear a robe in the service, let him bear in mind that there is good psychology in wearing clothes which help lift him out of the ranks of the ordinary everyday man into a helpful apartness which aids both his audience and himself. Light tan shoes and "loud" neckties, colored shirts and ten-cent-store socks, are positively not in order at the altar or in the pulpit.

2. WHEN THE MINISTER DRIVES A CAR

Placing an average man behind the steering wheel of a car does something to him; and, after all, the minister is usually an average man. Filling our roads with automobiles brought an ugly word back into frequent use. That unlovely word is just plain "hog." The road hog is by no means a rare creature. If you want to breed insolence in a man, try putting him in command at the steering wheel of a car—the bigger and higher-powered, the better—but any little old "flivver" will do.

The man behind the wheel is boss—until he sees a traffic officer. He can become very meek and law-abiding if he sees the officer in time, and very meek and submissive if he sees him too late.

The minister preaches respect for law and order. Does he include the laws and ordinances which govern motor-driven traffic on the highway? Let those of the cloth among us who always religiously observe these regulations rise and answer. To many a minister the rules of traffic on the highway are little more than dead letters. When a sign reads "Speed Limit 35 Miles," he drives 50. When a sign reads "No Parking at Any Time," he deliberately parks. He passes other cars on sharp curves. He neglects to signal his turns and stops to the motorist behind him. He makes a clearly forbidden U-turn. He assumes the right of way at an intersection although another car is reaching the intersection, coming from his right. He double-parks in any narrow street. He does all the careless tricks a heedless youth is known to do. As for an explanation, well, those signs and regulations are not meant to be taken seriously. He has his own interpretations. When a sign reads "35 Miles," that really means not over 45; when it reads "Slow," that means if the road is wet or icy, otherwise it means nothing; when it reads "Stop," that means slow down to about 15 miles. In short, all that the laws and the signs demand is that the driver, using his own judgment, be careful; and, as long as the minister deems that he is driving carefully enough, he is excusable. After all, is he not a minister of the gospel, and, as such, somewhat privileged?

I shall not hesitate to aver that some of the road signs are silly; but in the main they are justified; and I want to put it up squarely to the minister's conscience whether he does not almost daily take unwarranted liberties on the road. If his conscience will not make him circumspect, he is hopeless.

What happens when he is arrested and questioned by a traffic officer? Is he always strictly truthful in the explanations he makes of the affair? If he does not baldly fib, is he not often guilty of being somewhat economical with the truth? And has he any right whatsoever to mouth around about monumental injustice when, proved guilty, he is plastered with a sizable fine?

Here is another question. Is it strictly ethical for the minister to expect and accept preferential treatment at the hands of law-enforcing traffic officers? Shall he carry a "Clergy" insigne on his car, or wear clericals, in order to make himself immune? What entitles him to greater consideration on the highway than that accorded to any other driver? What of my clerical friend who, in a city where Roman Catholics are numerous and where the traffic officers are mostly of the same persuasion and never molest a priest, giggles when he tells me that in his clericals he looks so much like a Romanist priest that he may drive where and as he pleases without fear of detention?

I fear I have another count against the minister who drives a car. Many ministers are either constitutionally or habitually careless about any tools or machinery. The minister's saws and chisels and hatchet are usually rusted and dull. His lawn mower is not in prime condition. His wife can never get him to repair little things about the house or to tidy anything about the yard. This extends to his care of his car. But what if it does? If his car wears out faster than it should, if it uses more gasoline and oil than it should, if its brakes are unreliable, is it not his car to treat as he chooses? Wait a minute! That car, ill cared for, becomes a menace on the road. It is far more likely to figure in an accident than the car kept in A-1 condition. Has the careless minister any license to chug a menace to other people's limb and life along our roads?

I wonder how many ministers know that the appearance of their cars is almost as important as their own. If slovenliness in attire is unpardonable in the minister, what of slovenliness in the care of his car? I do not mean that he must always be driving the latest model. His financial situation may not allow a trade-in every year or two. But, whatever the year of his car, he can keep it clean within and without. The clutter which characterizes the interior of many a minister's car is positively not to be ignored, and the presence of layer upon layer of road splash on its exterior wins him nobody's respect. If he does not have the time or the means to keep his car clean, he should not have one.

This leads to another question. Are there not hundreds of parishes which could be well served by a minister without a car? Have we drifted into a supine acceptance of the opinion that, no matter how it strains our financial resources, we in the Ministry must all have cars? In the old horse-and-buggy days few city ministers had conveyances. Today so few ministers are without cars that their number is negligible. Are our parishes really being better served thereby, or is it that we are only taking life easier—or imagining we are? A load of constant automobile expense which keeps us just one jump ahead of the foreclosing officer surely is not calculated to make life easy and pleasant.

Some ministers are fortunate (?) enough to have parishes which buy the pastor's car, or pay for the gasoline and upkeep, or do both. I question their good fortune; for an arrangement of this kind produces plenty of unfavorable comment among the members of the parish. When the minister takes a pleasure trip, especially an extended one, or when his boys or his girls dash around town in the car, more than one caustic comment is heard. Better buy your own car and pay for its running and upkeep out of your own funds.

And, Brother, let me whisper this: do not let your car become a convenience bus or a delivery truck for the various nervy members of your parish. It is Christian to accommodate people; but it is not conducive to the welfare of the Kingdom to encourage church members to depend on their minister and his car to such an extent as to make him lose time and patience doing errand-boy jobs for audacious church members who are making a convenience of his car. All the more reason why the car and the gasoline should be his. But, whether or not, the minister who introduces the habit or allows it to grow lets himself in for all sorts of irritations and unfavorable criticism in the bargain. About the only reward he gets is the inane applause, "Oh, our minister is just the nicest man—he'll do anything for a person!"

3. WHEN THE MINISTER RECEIVES PRESENTS

The Bible has something alarming to say about accepting gifts. It is in Proverbs 15:27: "He that hateth gifts shall live [prosper]." To be sure, what is here condemned is the taking of bribes. But gifts to a minister, welcome though they may be, sorely needed sometimes, should be considered for their possible offer as bribes, or for the possibility they may be interpreted as bribes, however innocent the intentions of both giver and recipient may be.

I heard a minister say, when informed that a church had given its minister a beautiful, expensive automobile: "Well, I want that never to happen to me; for, just stop and think what that church will now expect of him; he will be so beholden to the members that he will be made miserable." Extreme as this sounds, there is something to what this brother said. There is something to the question whether even unpretentious gifts from the individual parishioner to the pastor may not work more embarrassment than pleasure. There was a day when ministers' salaries were so modest that they needed to be eked out by gifts, especially in rural parishes. Even in those days there were whispers that the minister called oftenest on the farmer who sent him on his homeward way with the most and the best produce in the back of his buggy.

Now, it so happens that in the Ministry equal treatment and consideration should by all means be extended by the minister to each of his members. He cannot be on equally cordial and intimate terms with all in the parish, for the simple reason that some church members are personally much more approachable and responsive than others. But woe to him when he gives cause for being justly charged with exercising partiality. It is immeasurably easier for him to escape being so charged if he is not placed under extra obligation to anyone through receiving gifts.

We have, I suppose, all known and at least mildly despised the minister who was an adept at hinting for gifts. Placed at a hospitable table in the home of one of his rural parishioners, hear him praise the excellent quality of the butter, the fruit or the sausage. His wife at home never gets a word of praise for her viands. Why waste his arts on her?

The subject of perquisites belongs in this chapter. A wide and emphatic difference of views prevails in regard to them.

Some people are so violently opposed to any defense of perquisites that they sarcastically call them tips. Others argue that special individual services rendered may fitly be recompensed with special remuneration. The government gives perquisites legal status by demanding that gifts received in recognition of services rendered must be included in one's income tax return for income tax payment on them.

Rendering certain individual services often puts the minister to considerable expense not only of time and energy but also of cash. When he incurs such expense, which may amount to a goodly number of dollars, by visiting sick people who live miles away, sometimes on poor roads, then officiating at the funeral, which may carry him to a cemetery still farther away, can anyone justly find fault with him for accepting compensation, or even, in the case of nonmembers, sending a bill if compensation is not forthcoming? "The laborer is worthy of his hire." "Thou shalt not muzzle the mouth of the ox that treadeth out the corn." Paul significantly asks, "Doth God take care for oxen?"

The one thing to be said to the minister is "Be cautious." It is going too far to say to the church member, "Thou shalt remember the pastor with special gifts." It is likewise going too far to say to the pastor, "Thou shalt not accept any gifts from individual members of thy parish." But it is not going too far to say to the minister, "Beware of laying thyself open to a just charge of being either a sponge or a gold digger." And it is not going too far to say to the church member what Scripture says, "Let him that is taught in the word communicate unto him that teacheth in all good things."

Gifts bestowed on the minister by his church as such or by an organization of his church are in a class different from those of the individual church member. It is eminently fitting to remember the pastor with a gift at Christmas time, on his birthday, on the occasions of the anniversaries of his ordination or his installation or his wedding; but the minister who is careful to hint for such remembrances by speaking of the events as the anniversaries approach is inviting harmful criticism. No matter how slyly and casually he (or his wife) may drop remarks about an approaching anniversary, the listeners will usually be keen enough to sense that the remarks are purposive.

Even worse is the habit of some ministers to show their displeasure at not receiving gifts by calling members' attention to the circumstance that a neighboring parish has bestowed a generous gift on its pastor, ending with the happy remark, "Those people certainly know how to treat their minister." Probably in nine cases out of ten the members' reaction to such a display of chagrin would, if spoken, take the form, "Well, Pastor, if you would make yourself as useful and as agreeable as he does, we'd open our hearts and our hands too."

Sometimes inappropriate or shoddy gifts reach the manse. Thanks for them, or at least for the spirit which prompted them, must be spoken, assuming that the giver had no intention of showing disrespect. Such thanks are not necessarily hypocritical, nor are they difficult when one follows the Christian obligation always to put the best construction on others' acts; but sometimes this is virtually impossible. Some good soul sends you an atrocious framed picture or a hideous piece of furniture. What to do with such gifts? Install them, and suffer day by day? What a temptation, especially to the minister's wife, to exhibit disappointment, not to say disgust! But— you'll be wise to make the best of it. Surely, you can find an inconspicuous place for the picture or the piece of furniture. As for other undesirable donations, after all you are not worse off when someone gives you a basketful of bruised windfalls, or a tough old hen, than you would be if nothing at all had been brought. One in the Ministry soon learns tact in how he, and his wife if he has one, can dispose of such gifts.

4. WHEN THE MINISTER ATTENDS A CONVENTION

A minister of my acquaintance failed to attend the annual convention of his district. The board of his parish had ruled that the week he would spend at the convention should be considered a part of his annual vacation. He disagreed so emphatically that the outcome was a mass of hurt and hard feelings, and his absence from that year's convention. Who is to blame for the prevailing opinion of many church members that ministers who attend conventions are taking a holiday? Perhaps many a minister himself is at fault.

It is positively true that sitting in a church convention six hours and more a day and keeping one's mind on the subjects discussed and the business transacted is exhausting labor. But we have the authentic picture of dozens of ministers who spend one whole day, either going to convention or returning home, on side trips to visit relatives or friends *on convention time.* We also have the true-to-life picture of dozens of ministers who spend an hour or two a day in the convention, and the remaining hours outside, indulging in conversations with other loafing brethren. I have often wondered why such ministers do not comprehend what a sorry impression their conduct makes on lay delegates who behold it. It is not strange that in some places a minister's solemn remarks about his convention duties raise the shoulders of his knowing parishioners in a shrug.

Ministers have other bad convention habits. Many of them quite regularly neglect attendance at the devotions which open every session. Conduct they themselves severely reprove in their parishioners at home seems entirely excusable in themselves at conventions. Let it be admitted that a considerable part of the benefit of attending a convention is to be found in the contacts for which the gathering furnishes opportunity—such social contacts do not have the right of way.

Further: a habit which the average minister unsparingly and unremittingly condemns in the home church is the unbreakable determination of many of his parishioners to occupy only the rear seats in his church. Time after time he fulminates against this objectionable practice. But, when he is at convention, he planks himself into a seat as far removed from the chairman's desk as he can find. He would sit in the very last

row if it were not for the deplorable circumstance that this
row is already filled by like-minded ministers who have beat
him to it.

Has there ever been a church convention at which the clos-
ing session had more than a bare quorum present to transact
its business? Has a minister any right to accept transportation
expense to attend a convention, then merely for personal inclination leave a day or two before the adjournment? Oh, the
heap of excuses ministers have minted, why they could not
possibly stay to the close! And yet they expect people to
respect them as honest, conscientious men!

5.   WHEN THE MINISTER GOES ON VACATION

Certainly, the minister should have vacations. He should
have them regularly. If he is timid about taking them or (as
is the case with some natures) averse to them, he should be
compelled to take them. Years ago there was a story in circulation to the effect that in a church of pious, gospel-hardened
people the minister was finally by resolution granted a vacation. Next day after the meeting one of his reputedly devout
members, who had opposed the resolution, met him with the
dolorous remark, "But, Pastor, the Devil never takes a vacation." The minister had the quick wit to respond, "Brother, if
the Devil had as hard a job as I have taking care of you, he
would have closed shop long ago."

Emphatically, the minister needs periods of total release
from the strain of his trying duties in order to relax and be
refreshed. It is a sign of advance, that most churches grant
regular vacations on full pay, and also provide for the needed
supplies during such vacations. It is to be hoped that ministers
will be discreet enough not to allow discredit to come on
themselves and on the entire vacation question by vacation
conduct which must be disapproved.

There is undeniably a human tendency which prompts people, when the restraints which ordinarily bind them are

slackened, to act as though they were loose to do as they willfully please. The minister is not without human weaknesses. Let loose from the inhibitions of his regulated routine, he is in danger of making entirely too much of his liberty.

The highway speed limit may mean nothing to him. Along the road he may stop at refreshment places, the like of which he would not think of entering in his home town. He may get free and breezy with comely waitresses, slangy with filling-station men. Often he does not care how he looks. He may get far too gay on the bathing beach. He may play the slot machines, in spite of the lectures he has often given his people at home against gambling. He may smoke too much, eat too much, stay up until the small hours of the morning. It is perfectly proper for him on vacation to be a boy again; but is it necessary for him to be a bad boy, or a boy without good breeding, in order to have a good time? Is there any good reason why the minister away from home should be entirely different in conduct from the minister at home? Do all sorts of indulgences send him home from vacation really refreshed, really strengthened for the months which lie ahead?

Should the minister preach in others' pulpits while he is on vacation? It is best for him not to do so unless he can do so without much effort; and this, with the minister to whom every sermon he delivers should be a heavy responsibility, is hardly possible. No brother minister is dealing fairly when he insists that a minister taking a vacation in his vicinity preach for him. To be sure, preaching the Sunday morning sermon is far from being the only work the minister has to do. Even if he delivers a Sunday sermon while away, he is getting a vacation from all the other tasks and worries and vexations. Just the same, preaching for others while he is on vacation is not fair either to himself or to his home congregation; and, if he yields and, in order not to exert himself, preaches a lackadaisical sermon, it is not fair to the afflicted congregation.

How long to stay on vacation? Not less than three Sundays a year, making the total of days about four weeks. In rare cases the minister may be fortunate enough to receive a year for a foreign tour or other extended trip.

Whether long or short, the minister should remember that his vacation should be just what the word says, a cancelation of his work and worry schedule. He should not leave home promising to return in case of someone's sickness; nor should he promise to write every family in the parish a post card or two. Let him unload everything and forget about his congregation and fill his days with delicious obliviousness. Only so can he return with a good conscience, feeling that in granting him his vacation his congregation has made a good investment.

Let me add that I have always failed to see how a minister can, unless there are unusual circumstances, go on vacation with a good conscience without taking his wife and children along. I am speaking of vacations, not of convalescents' furloughs. The minister may not stop to think of it; but let me tell him that a large proportion of his membership will gossip about him as just another selfish man if he goes away to enjoy a change and leaves his family to the monotony of its routine. It is likewise imprudent for the shepherd and the shepherdess to take their vacations apart from each other. I have not one moment's tolerance for the philosophy that it is good for husband and wife to "enjoy" a change from constant companionship with each other. The pastor and his wife should be a convincing illustration that in all ways and at all times "the twain shall be one." Pastors complain about gossip. Well, gossip arises often anent the preacher's relation to his wife and their conduct toward each other.

As for the "delicate" preacher's assertion that he is "nervous" and must get away from the racket raised by his children, I have but one word of comment, and that one word is "Ridiculous!"

Chapter 5

THE MINISTER'S BUSINESS MATTERS

1. WHEN THE MINISTER NEEDS MORE MONEY

These lines are being written at a time when high prices for all commodities, as also high taxes, which distress the pocketbook of even the low-salaried minister, are making me wonder how thousands of ministers are able to manage at all. The minister's pocketbook needs serious and kindly attention. But this is true in most periods. The churches have suffered greatly because of their usual habit of supplying their ministers with too little of the coin of the realm. Many of the jibes at the minister and many of the caricatures of him on the stage, in books, and in the comic (?) strips never would have been plausible had the average minister not been compelled to act the role of those whose position demands far more in the way of funds than is provided.

It will probably always be the rule that the Ministry is largely recruited from social strata in which frugality must be constantly practiced. It requires little experience with human nature to know that the incessant practice of thrift, while it has its use in toughening certain fibers of character, also carries with it injuries to some of those elements of a person's makeup which would broaden him and build up in him a certain air of confidence which is a valuable asset in life. To spend one's childhood and then go through college and seminary only a step or two "ahead of the sheriff" does more harm than good to the prospective prophet of God. To enter the Ministry on a low salary and with school debts on his shoulders is to invite the danger either that he will have "his style cramped," or that he will be compelled to rob himself of needed helps or resort to "schemes" in order to make ends meet. He will be too obsequious toward his financially well-fixed parishioners and fellow townsmen, he will be too cautious when marketing for the parsonage table—in other words, he will be to his neighbors "Poor Mr. Smith—how does he get along?" Instead of heading this discussion, "When the Minister Needs More Money," let us phrase it, "The Minister Needs More Money, That's Plain."

This being the case, what shall he do about it? The pity is that, if anything is to be done, it is so often left to him to do it. How he, unless he is mercenarily inclined, dislikes to initiate proceedings looking toward a betterment of his financial status! Plainly the straightforward and honorable step for him to take is to place the matter in a businesslike way before the officers of his parish, or before a selected discreet few of them, or before their chief officer. This had best not be the treasurer. Church treasurers are, I would prefer not to feel I have to say it, very often not so willing to part with funds as to receive and hold them. They make themselves watchdogs of the funds, rather than administrators of them; and their proclivity to be watchdogs places many of them in the bulldog class, with a very tenacious grip on the funds entrusted to them. They rarely favor having the parish assume new financial obligations. For this reason the minister who needs more money had better confer with some other influential parish officer or officers.

Some parishes actually expect the minister to earn additional money "on the side." If he can do this in the direction of his calling, there is little objection. If the minister can earn an honest dollar by delivering lectures, by writing for periodicals, by the authorship of books, he is killing several birds with one stone: adding to his income and disseminating cultural and missionary material, while also improving himself mentally. But, when he is expected to drive a school bus, to take a position as teacher in the public school, to farm, to raise poultry, and the like, he is making a mistake by complying. The money he earns is more than offset by the loss his parish suffers, and by the almost inevitable lowering of his self-respect or of the dignity of his office.

Sometimes the minister needs money in an unusual emergency. The only recourse is to borrow. Now, although I have said that borrowing and sorrowing are closely akin, there are circumstances under which borrowing simply must be done. In such cases let the minister go directly to his banker and state his case.

The minister should not "play the stock market" in the hope of adding to his financial resources. Need I enumerate the reasons? Nor should he enter the real estate business to get more money. There are too many pitfalls, and strict honesty is hard to maintain in business transactions; and, even when a real estate dealer is upright and has not given false impressions, he will invariably have customers who feel that they have a grievance. A minister entering any kind of business lays himself open to fault-finding and other grief.

The real answer to the minister's money questions is for the general church bodies to decide on a fair salary minimum, then for individual churches to live up to the established scale, preferably to exceed it.

2. WHEN THE MINISTER BORROWS

There is an old saying that "borrowing begets sorrowing." A stern truth is expressed in this trite utterance, and it has stood the test of centuries. But, like other pat sayings, it asserts too much. To take borrowing out of present-day life would be inconceivable—impossible. Much of our interlacing economy proceeds on the assumption that there will be borrowing. There may be a few self-confident rugged individuals who still, usually with much smirking self-satisfaction, claim that they never borrow. Let us not begrudge them their complacency. As surely as they are part and parcel of present-day society, they are indebted to countless borrowing predecessors and contemporaries, whether they themselves have contracted aboveboard loans or not. One cannot live today without being a borrower, a reaper where others have planted, a builder on foundations laid by others.

But most of us are direct borrowers, and we have no good reason to be ashamed of this. The honest borrower is as honorable a person as anyone needs to be. This matter is being discussed here, not to condemn the minister if he borrows, but to keep him wise, honest and honorable if and when he does.

There comes to mind the solemn advice of a hoary seminary professor when we were divinity students: "If it becomes necessary for you to borrow money, do not borrow from a member of your parish, but rather go to an 'outsider.'" Was that good advice? Yes—and no. It is easy to see how, having borrowed money from his church member, a minister may feel under more than financial obligation to this member. There is large danger of interference with his laudable intention to treat all of his church members alike. Somehow, even when a minister is paying good interest on borrowed money, he is inclined to feel that he has been made a beneficiary by the person extending him the loan.

Other considerations claim attention. Many a borrower of money, perhaps oftenest a borrowing minister, has overestimated his ability to refund the loan. Or, a lender who thought that he could conveniently spare the money indefinitely, may easily, by reason of changed circumstances, discover that he needs his money back much sooner than he had calculated. It is not difficult to visualize the many embarrassments which can enter when the transaction has been between minister and member.

On the other hand, embarrassments equally vexing may arise if the minister borrows money from an individual who is not a member of his parish. The very step of divulging to an "outsider" that one needs money is not a desirable one to take. Shall an "outsider" be told that the minister's parish does not sufficiently remunerate him to enable him to meet his legitimate expenses? Shall the "outsider" be made to feel that the minister must go outside the circle of his own parishioners to find a friend in need? One thing is certain: the minister, when he feels justified to borrow, should be extremely cautious. Let him weigh all the probabilities and possibilities before he decides where to apply for a loan.

One solution of the problem is for the minister not to borrow money from any individual, but to go to his bank and apply for a loan there. Banks are in the business of making loans. To be sure, the banker may advise the minister against making the contemplated loan; but, when he does, the advice is usually not only sound but also well meant. The legend of the heartless, steel-eyed banker is just that—not much more. Many a minister would today have the money he lost in imprudent ventures if he had listened to the advice of the local banker.

The innumerable warnings which have been issued regarding loan "sharks" may well be heeded by the minister, although the danger is now not so great as formerly. Their circulars are enticing, their offers seem attractive, and their willingness to lend is flattering. The lists of ministers' addresses are easily obtained, and the minister who does not toss third-class mail into the wastebasket unopened is constantly reading circular letters, often with his name typed in to make the "coaxer" seem personal, offering to lend him money on ridiculously easy monthly refunds; the whole transaction, of course, to be fully confidential. I took the time and trouble once to figure out a particularly alluring offer. One could have, for the mere asking (and signing), $100 up to $300. On the loan of $100 for one year one was to pay only $10.30 a month for twelve months. Now, paying back a loan of this kind in monthly installments means actually having the use of only half the amount for the year. At $10.30 a month, the borrower would pay a total of $123.60; or $23.60 more than the $100 he secured. Plainly, $23.60 is 47⅕ per cent on $50. In other words, the highly favored borrower was to pay that exorbitant interest. The only borrower who can afford to pay interest of such proportions is the borrower who can re-invest the loan at 50 per cent—and that is not the average minister. A loan shark is a shark, no matter what attractive name he may give himself, This-or-That Credit Association, This-or-That Finance Corporation, or what-have-you. That same loan for $100 at the bank at 6 per cent on renewable sixty-day notes would cost only $6, which is 12 per cent on $50.

Installment buying is a form of borrowing. There is always an admitted or a concealed carrying charge. The system has become so fixed and respectable an arrangement, welcomed and encouraged by virtually all large firms and corporations, that it would be silly for me to decry its practice. Many a family owns a home it never could have secured as its own if it had not been allowed to pay for it while occupying it. Few people have ever paid cash for their automobiles. And, while the practice seems badly overdone when clothing and house furnishings of every description are bought "on lease," basi-cally and logically there is no difference, no matter what the purchase may be.

But it is easy to see that the practice has led to the virtual mortgaging of thousands of people's incomes far in advance of their earning them. Shall the minister join the endless pro-cession, buying almost everything he needs, and everything he and his family want, on the installment plan? It would be idle for him to imagine that he alone could effect a revolution in this matter of general merchandising by refraining from buying except for cash. At the same time he can, I believe, purchase for himself a large quantity of peace of mind by going slowly on lease commitments. More than that, it is not the installment-plan buyer who gets real bargains. It takes cash for these, and the inveterate installment-plan buyer just does not have available cash—ever.

Another form of borrowing which concerns the minister is running store accounts. Of course the minister has credit at the store. Almost any firm will sell to him on account. There are also some substantial advantages in being a charge customer, especially at the big department store. Unfair as it may seem, this big concern extends more favors and courtesies to the charge customer than to the cash patron.

I have known ministers and others who took particular pride and apparently felt more virtuous because they planked down cash for every purchase; no account at the grocery, at the meat market, at the drug store, even at the doctor's, paying him visit by visit. I have no quarrel with these people; nor with those who prefer to run accounts. But I do want to say that the minister who does have charge accounts must keep his credit good and his reputation sound by living up strictly to the regulations of the firms which carry his account. It is a discredit not only to the minister, but to the Ministry, to have him carelessly ignore the obligations of the store account.

One of the fruitful fields of the professional jester is the neighborhood borrowing habit. Here is a December cartoon, showing a boy returning a borrowed lawn mower and at the same time asking for the loan of the neighbor's snow shovel. Some neighbors borrow eggs, butter, tea, sugar, garden hose, kettles, etc.; and many have the reputation of seldom remembering that they have borrowed. There are neighbors who borrow eggs in January when they cost ninety cents a dozen, and return the loan in April when eggs cost much less. There are neighbors who borrow a car with the tank full of gasoline and return it with the tank one-fourth full, and fender scratched or dented.

Where do the minister and his family come into this picture? I fear they often line up as forgetful neighbors in the activity of borrowing promiscuously and returning fitfully.

Some ministers' transgressions in borrowing and not returning have to do with books. They borrow them freely, and books, somehow, have a way of remaining unreturned, even after the lender has made repeated inquiries about them. "The wicked borroweth, and payeth not again" (Psalm 37:21).

3. WHEN THE MINISTER HANDLES OTHERS' MONEY

It would be better if the minister in the average church did not need to concern himself about finances—his own and those of the church. I have heard this said countless times through the years of my ministry; but in our circles little change has been effected in this regard, and probably little will be. Ministers are still in large part inadequately salaried and still have to worry about making the ends of their family budgets meet. Moreover, church members are still slow in responding to the demands of their own congregational budgets, as also to the requirements of what is usually called Benevolence. In many churches, if the minister did not either take it upon himself or allow himself to be commandeered, the financial condition of his church would be in sad condition as to both local and general requirements. It is often the minister who must be concerned to keep the parish credit good and its benevolent contributions at least somewhat respectable.

Connected with this part of church work is the frequent employment of the minister as receiver and disburser of funds. Were he to evade service of this kind, the gifts for church work would often be less than they are. People have the habit of giving him contributions for various purposes. They have deep confidence in him as the proper agent for their benevolence—or is it that they want to make sure that he knows that they are giving goodheartedly, and just how generous they are? In many parishes, too, the minister is asked to procure Bibles and other books and to attend to church-paper subscriptions.

Again and again ministers have had sorry experiences when

they thus handled other people's money. The only safe line of performance is strict business administration of entrusted funds. Giving and taking receipts, regular bookkeeping entries, audits and the like are good safeguards. Even with them the minister is constantly liable to be suspected. He should as much as possible avoid handling other people's money.

There have been cases in which ministers were asked to invest entrusted funds, and in which they acted conscientiously in what appeared to them to be the best interests of the would-be investors, only to see the investments take wing and fly away. I knew a minister who skimped and saved for years to make good some investments of this kind, and he was completely innocent of any dishonest appropriation of his parishioners' funds, having followed their wishes in the choice of investment.

As for the minister who solicits funds for investment in some project which he has invented or which he chooses to advance for others, being certain that the investment is sound, my unhesitating advice is, "Don't!" It may occur that a deep and righteous interest in one's community and its prosperity will suggest that the minister enter into the financial operation of a community enterprise. I have known cases in which the minister became promoter of local business projects to increase employment and thus keep young people from deserting the old home town. I have known no case in which the minister did not come to grief in such effort.

Should the minister accept the trust of becoming executor or administrator of members' estates? He is often asked to do this. I think some ministers have "hinted themselves" into employment in this line. I knew a minister who accepted the position of administrator of a widow's estate. He had attended her for years in her sickness; she had confided to him the unfriendly feelings of her children toward each other. She feared her ne'er-do-well son would cause trouble. The minister was asked to see that the little estate be administered as she wished, and he helped her word her will. Not long after her death the son threatened to shoot the minister if he dared set foot on the property. Unscared, he did set foot on it and there faced the son—and was not shot—and is alive today to tell the tale. But his church members were so much alarmed that they induced him to resign as administrator and ask the court to appoint someone else. Their advice was probably good.

In conclusion, let me advise the minister to keep his participation in the handling of others' money at the least possible minimum.

4.   WHEN THE MINISTER OWNS REAL ESTATE

The average minister occupies a manse, or a parsonage. He does not need to provide a house for himself. But there are many cases in which his dwelling is a rented house, the rent being paid either for him or to him by his parish. Renting is a transaction which has so many drawbacks that the minister who lives in rented quarters is tempted to buy a property; and some ministers have yielded to the temptation.

A minister soon discovers, however, that, desirable as it is to own one's home, ownership has its multitude of cares and annoyances. The upkeep of real property, plus payment of installments, interest, insurance and taxes, is not child's play.

What to do—rent or buy? The question grows more frequent. In old down town sections there are parishes whose manses are located in neighborhoods which have become so shabby that it is unwholesome for the minister and his family to live there. More than a few ministers, unable to persuade their parishes to secure manses in more desirable locations, have chosen to rent or to buy elsewhere on their own.

One difficulty, when the minister owns his home, is that this influences him considerably in deciding whether at a given time to remain with his parish or to accept a transfer elsewhere. Desirable as it sometimes is for a parish to have a change in its pastorate, the minister may remain because there is no ready sale for his property; or, if sold, no proper return on investment; or because, if he departs and rents his property, he will need the services and be required to pay the commission of an agent, besides having the annoyance of meeting the demands of a captious tenant.

Another difficulty enters when the minister, having bought a property on contract, is unable to meet the payments and hold his purchase. No matter what the circumstances may be, his credit will be unfavorably affected if he is sold out under a foreclosed mortgage. Imprudent as some preachers are in business matters, this might happen. Look well before you leap into a property purchase.

Some ministers inherit property, or get into its possession through marriage. They certainly cannot then be held at fault for owning it. But, as landlords, they will be almost certain to incur much of the odium usually visited upon owners who rent to others. It will be an exceptionally tactful or haply a fortunate minister who escapes the ugly criticisms which renters and their sympathizers have in store in large measure for those who control rental properties. Even though the average renter is both exacting and destructive, he is usually considered the underdog and gets the neighborhood's sympathy.

Shall the minister who happens to have extra funds to invest acquire and sell property on speculation? Most ministers are opposed to all speculation, calling it gambling; but, somehow, by a twist of moral ratiocination, they manage to exclude real estate deals from the category of disapproved transactions. Has the minister a moral right to buy property with the idea of cashing in a handsome profit when it increases in value and he sells it at a big advance? Has he the time to devote to real estate manipulations? Has he the physical vigor to remain unaffected when the real estate market gets shaky? Paul told Timothy that the love of money is the root of all kinds of evil. The minister who speculates in property does it because he wants more money. He is on dangerous ground.

Shall the minister own real property? He certainly may if

he can and if he so chooses. But he will need a special measure of grace to keep out of mischief and free of heartaches. Annoyances multiply since so much is expected of the property owner. A petition will circulate for street paving, sewer extension, and the like. A neighbor may want a line fence which the minister considers unnecessary. The telephone company will want to lop tree limbs from favorite trees and protest must be made. I once plagiarized and published a couplet for ministers:

> *From money and from property,*
> *Good Lord, deliver us!*

That was in a sense absurd; but at the time a number of my fellow ministers had gone into a property-buying deal, expecting to colonize church members in a new territory and clean up a sizable profit. They ran into difficulties, made only negligible financial margins, lost time and face; and I wanted to give them a gentle reproof in that couplet.

I thoroughly dislike the epithet, "The poor preacher," when it is currently used to signify that the preacher is poor in this world's goods. It has hurt the Church to have its leaders habitually considered men of tattered coats and frayed shirts. But the remedy is not the vesting of property rights in the minister. After all, the Master was pitifully poor throughout the years of His visible bodily presence on earth, and it was out of his own experience that Paul wrote to a young preacher that reminder about the root of all kinds of evil. And Paul added, after recounting the evils, "Thou, O man of God, flee these things"!

For one reason or another, the "well fixed" minister is usually at a disadvantage. He will have many members in his parish who, just because he is better situated as to property than they are, allow their feelings toward him to be tinged with envy. He will be deprived of many of the comforting attentions which solicitous church members usually accord their shepherd. He will find himself strangely at a loss when

he is attempting to console or encourage those who are struggling with difficulties with which he has never needed to
contend. They will, he senses, be saying in their hearts, "It is
easy for him to tell us just to pray and to trust in the Lord.
He isn't in our boat—he hasn't a thing to worry about—he's
sittin' pretty."

Nevertheless, after all this has been said, I believe no one
will find fault with the minister who, by frugality and thrift
(not miserliness), can look forward to declining years for
which, instead of "living around" with his married children,
he has provided a modest little home for himself and his life
companion. Fair-minded people will, rather, commend him for
having been thrifty.

Chapter 6

THE MINISTER'S PASTORAL RELATIONS

1. WHEN THE MINISTER GREETS PEOPLE

Always the minister's sincerity is under suspicion by many of those who come in contact with him. This is to be expected. Most people are by nature suspicious: but any man whose very profession and whose constant preachments make their consciences uneasy must be prepared to incur their specially keen observation and their persistent mistrust—indicated by the shrug of shoulders, if nothing more.

An activity of the minister most frequently laid in the balance of invidious examination is his exercise of friendliness. The minister who remains ever sedate and uneffusive is criticized for his lack of human warmth. The minister who always has a sparkle in his eye and a handshake for everyone he meets is criticized for his excessive pretensions of geniality. The minister who plans to escape such criticism is doomed to disappointment; the one who attempts to prove that his cordiality is sincere is engaged in a recommended effort.

First of all, he should be lovingly sincere in his attentions to all. That, you observe, "goes without saying." No, it does not. He is as other folks. No one can really enjoy encounters with those trying people whom we call bores. Every church has at the least one; and the minister is the favorite victim, because, for good reason, he has to stand still and look pleasant while being bored. I am firmly convinced that the Recording Angel does not make an entry on the debit side of the minister's ledger when, seeing a bore at a distance, the minister ducks in somewhere or crosses the street in order to avoid a meeting. Just the same, when a meeting is inescapable, the minister must be sincerely friendly. True sincerity will in season win general recognition.

In the next place, the minister should temper his show of friendliness, not allowing it ever to drip or to ooze, to bubble or to froth; but, on the other hand, he should not repress cordiality of manner in order, as he judges, to keep it within the bounds of studied dignity. Cultivating a genuine friendliness toward all, he may safely leave it to his feelings when he meets and greets people to find the proper manner and degree of affability. To say of a preacher, referring to his greetings, that "he is always the same" is not a compliment. He should not be a stereotype. He should be different when occasions and personalities differ.

The handshake is generally accepted to be one of the minister's indispensable performances. When I was a young man I was reserved and distant in manner. A successful minister, several years my senior, was my guest preacher one Sunday. After we had left the church he frankly said to me, "Walter, you don't shake hands enough." I thought he was right; and, indeed, later I knew he was; and I owe him my thanks for correcting me. Yet, there is such a thing as shaking hands too much. A handshake loses some of its impressiveness when it is made an indiscriminate performance.

Better not shake hands if you do not do it properly. I have people shake hands with me, and I get the sensation of being in touch with a limp dead snake. Some ministers forget themselves when shaking hands with women, and their clasp is so vigorous that they inflict pain. I think the minister may with all propriety follow the Emily Post rule that a man not shake a woman's hand unless and until she offers it. Then let him refrain from being too athletic.

2.   WHEN THE MINISTER IS IN SOCIETY

There is no denying that gloss counts for much in many people's estimation; and there is no denying that often it is not only superficial but has nothing beneath it to be valued or admired. Sham has become closely associated with so-called polite society in many people's opinion. This may be a reason why we have always had ministers who, instead of acquiring the gloss while retaining the gold, have affected brusqueness of speech and manner. They have been pleased to term their rudeness sincerity and frankness.

Now, there is such a quality as genuine and admirable personal politeness; and the minister should be the last man on earth to condemn or ignore it. The circumstance that others flash paste or brass should not prevent the minister from displaying some polish and sparkle in manner and speech. Boorishness is boorishness, even when practiced by men who have won their spurs. The little niceties of polite society should be habitual with the minister. Grace in speech and manner is worth while; let the minister recognize and cultivate it. Society needs men of character who can conform to its patterns and yet avoid its foibles and wickednesses. The minister could supply the deficiency.

Apart from this, he may well ask himself whether he dare risk losing the good opinion, especially of the young element in his community, by letting them think and say, "He doesn't know any better," when he leaves his spoon in his coffee cup, partakes of soup noisily, or bites into a whole slice of bread. To appear at dinner coatless, to interrupt someone who is speaking, or to laugh immoderately loud are also breaches of generally accepted etiquette.

As I have said before, there is much merriment in certain circles about Emily Post; but she is a lady trained in the requirements of polite society and is, moreover, in *Who's Who*, as most of us ministers are not. She was on radio for years;

many ministers get there seldom, or not at all. Over one hundred and fifty papers have carried her column daily, but not our column. We have much to gain and nothing to lose by being Chesterfieldian—in modification. Elegance of deportment is no mean asset, in whatever circles the minister moves.

Does good breeding require that the minister join in the drinking which is so regular a feature of society doings, both at table and before and after? It is well known that opinions on the use of alcoholic beverages differ among ministers. Some take the stand that no one, whether clergyman or layman, should ever use anything alcoholic as a beverage. Positive total abstinence, they maintain, is the only safe course and more, the only Scriptural and Christian course. Others as resolutely insist that the whole question is one of personal religious liberty, and of giving or taking offense. I need not repeat the arguments at length. Let this be said: no minister is required by any rule of polite society to join in even the most moderate drinking, if he feels bound by his conscience, or by sundry considerations to decline.

But, should he refuse to be a guest at a function because he knows beforehand that alcoholic drinks will be served? This is for him to decide. One thing is clear to me: if he declines invitations on this account, he should be man enough to make his reason plainly known. Is he morally upright when he invents excuses for not accepting them? Is he then better than if he accepts?

This brings up the question of society fibs—white lies, as they are inappropriately called. If a statement or an act is a lie, it cannot be white. We stand firm, most of us, on the assertion that the end never justifies the means; but hundreds of us make exceptions of lies told, as is alleged, for good purposes. There is just one honest and safe course: either tell the truth or be silent. I extend this even to the regulation falsehood, "Mrs. Smith, thank you for a very pleasant evening!" (Shall I add, "Pastor, I enjoyed your sermon very much this morning"?) You know, and probably Mrs. Smith knows, that you were bored to exasperation.

This reminds me that I have said nothing in this chapter about that ubiquitous creature, the society bore. How shall the minister treat him, or her? First of all, I ask the minister to make sure that he himself is not the bore. A hostess who had taken particular pains to arrange a delightful evening for us told my wife the next day that all evening I had acted like a bump on a log. She was right. I knew that one of her main objectives that evening was to parade me before some of her special friends who were not of our church—she was that proud of me. Now, I frankly confess that one of my chief abhorrences is to be "shown off." I acted as I did intentionally. Just the same, I afterwards regretted my boorishness, and I know that I profited by her correct and caustic thrust. The minister should never be justly accused of being a bore. This does not mean that he should go to the opposite extreme and exert himself to be the "life of the party."

As for other society bores—well—"What can't be cured must be endured." The minister is, it seems to me, oftener than most others the victim of the bore's steady relentless attacks. He is expected to be so tolerant and long-suffering that he does not execute even the proverbial worm's turn. The serious aspect of the experience is that usually this bore is keeping him from other desirable contacts. I advise him to acquire a technique in which there is enough "rudeness" to enable him to escape, and enough tact to prevent a justifiable charge of "cruelty to animals."

3.   When the Minister Converses

With all the caustic criticism of the garrulous, the verbose, the prolix and the loquacious, the fact remains that one of the finest accomplishments in which intelligent human beings can engage is conversation. We are not the only creatures with voices, but we are the only earthly species that can talk. I make no apology to parrot, magpie, starling or raven when I say this. I am referring to talk, not chatter and cackle.

Good conversationalists are held in high esteem, or they are not. This of course depends on the listener. Listening and speaking are equally important. In the true sense of the term, both are arts.

The minister is expected, rightly, to be a good conversationalist. I do not mean that he must be well posted on every phase of life's activities. No matter what the topic, politics, national or international; economics, industrial or occupational; events, literary or historical, some ministers jump into the conversation with an air of being versed in all the intricacies of the subject. I have little use for the minister who is either so absorbed in the technicalities of dogmatic theology, or so out of step with the ordinary folks, that he is ill at ease, and often positively dumb, when human affairs are under consideration. As stated elsewhere, the parson is no longer The Person, except in a very few isolated communities, but he should still be a man who is not tight-lipped while others are expressing themselves, and who is not uninformed in regard to many of the complex movements of men's minds and energies. He should be able to converse acceptably on dozens of subjects, and to use the speech which is current in circles not scholarly.

He should at the same time feel inclined to do so. Refusing to be interested in what interests other people, and loving lethargy too much to put oneself out a little by joining in current conversation, may rob the minister of a visa into the confidence and esteem of those whose friendship would be a decided acquisition at some later time. In order to avoid being a chattering magpie the minister need not shrink into the opposite extreme of making a clam of himself.

There has been much debate of what the minister may profitably talk about while he is making pastoral visits. Some have drawn a line of sharp demarcation between pastoral and social visits. I refuse to recognize the distinction. A visit is not necessarily pastoral because the minister insists on discussing matters of the soul and its welfare; nor is it necessarily social because he neglects to do this directly. As long as he comports himself as the pastor, what he says will be pastoral in effect, no matter what the subject may be. I do not want the young people of the family to feel impelled to say, "Our minister is a good sport," "A swell guy," "He knows his way around," or "He's as good as a circus"; but neither do I want them to have to blurt out, "Well, ministers are green ducks, aren't they?" or "Oh, I guess he means well!"

I wish I felt it unnecessary to say that the minister should never be a gossip. But the charge still persists that this and that minister knows everybody's business and carries things around from house to house on his rounds of visitation. When St. James calls the tongue "an unruly evil, full of deadly poison," I wish that I could feel certain that he did not have any minister's tongue in mind.

The gossiping minister is at his best when he is in conversation with fellow preachers about fellow preachers. It is astonishing, what unfounded reports about other ministers some ministers can peddle to their fellows. No one asks them, when they meet or gather socially, to spend the time "talking shop." Let them be human: let them relax. But God pity them if they think that having a good time away from their professional responsibilities means a feast of tattling and suspicion-mongering at the expense of their brothers in the Ministry.

One of the difficult conversational tasks of the minister is when he greets his congregation at the church doors after services. Few ministers attach much relevance to the perfunctory praises which are sung of them to them at such times (I hope). People do like to say something more than "Good morning!" especially since it is usually past the noon hour. So they tell the preacher that they enjoyed his sermon. What is he to answer?

How can he in the few seconds say something fitting to the member who has just recovered from sickness, or has lately been bereaved by a death, or has had some other trying ex-

perience? What can he say, in a hurried word or two, to
strangers to make them feel that he is really interested in
them? Or how impress the young fellows that going to church
is actually worth their while? I have repeatedly said that it
would be easier to preach a second sermon than to speak to
departing church attendants in words which will be like "a
golden apple laid on silver network" (Moffatt). But, Brother,
it is worth trying. Yet, remember that what you really have
to say to these people should have been said in your sermon.

One more warning in regard to the minister's conversation:
when he converses with his wife at home on church members
and church affairs, let it always—not merely usually, but
always—be with none of the children within hearing, no matter how young they may be. "Little pitchers have big ears."
And little pitchers may do a lot of spilling.

4. WHEN THE MINISTER MEETS CHILDREN

One of the sad circumstances in church life is that there are
gospel ministers who "have no use" for children. Their Master
loved the little ones. He took them up in His arms and blessed
them. He set them in the midst and asked His "seminarians" to
learn of them. I shall allow that there are many boys and girls
today who are not personally lovable, not in any sense admirable. I think that sensible home training of children by their
parents passed out before the home itself went by the board.
But I believe that under these circumstances our Lord would
say, "If ye are interested in only those children who are lovable, what thank have ye?"

I turn from the minister who has no use for children to the
minister who pretends that he is fascinated by them. Smiles
flood his face whenever he meets them. Baby lingo flows from
his honeyed lips. He can outdo the politician in chucking
babies under their chins. There may be a few fond mothers
whom he can fool; but let me tell him that, unless his interest
is genuine, boys and girls will see through him without fail.

If his interest is sincere, it will not evidence itself in overdone attention.

The minister who gives careful study to his contacts with children does wisely. The child fills a remarkably important and significant place in the world's life and in the sphere of its own community. It would be unpardonable if I failed to add the truism that the boys and girls of today are the men and women of the near future, and the equally trite proverb, "As the twig is bent, so the tree is inclined." The prudent minister will not ignore the child; and he will take an intelligent interest in all children, not only when he meets them, but when planning his work.

He meets the child in the home, on the street, in the store, at the ball game. This child is not constitutionally at war with the adult. It is to be regretted that many a preacher's ineptitude in accosting the child has given, especially to the average boy, a rather peculiar impression of the preacher, as have also the preacher's sermons. This circumstance adds to the difficulties of the situation. But the rewards of the minister's winning the good will and esteem of the child are so abundant and so rich that understanding must somehow be negotiated. The average child is so unerring in forming its estimate of humankind that the way of the minister into its respect will not be unduly hard to travel, provided the minister is honest.

Preacher, be genuinely, not artificially, interested in the children of your parish. Ponder their preciousness. Be aware of their potentialities. God has put immeasurably much into them. Study your way into the child's world. All this will banish the attitude of condescension to youth. See in the formative period of a child's life the field of your readiest opportunity to influence the course of human history. There is a skill which will make the toughest rowdy in the neighborhood respect and like the parson.

The minister meets, or by all means should meet, the child in the Sunday School. Opinions seem to differ on the question of the minister's duties and responsibilities in connection with this department. Some say, let him turn it over to a good superintendent. Others, let him confine his activity in the Sunday School to the adult Bible Class. I say, let him be known, heard and admired by every pupil in the school. I say this, well knowing from experience what a large order it is, but believing that it can be arranged, even though the minister may not see all the pupils every Sunday.

There are a few children whom the minister will meet in conducting the church service. Possibly there would be more of these if the sermon were so constructed and implemented that it held more appeal for the child mind. Long experience has inclined me to the opinion that no sermon can be contrived which will in all its expressions and content appeal to both the adult and the child. But neither can any sermon be contrived which will in like manner appeal to all the adults in one's audience. More should not be required or attempted than to present a sermon from which all present, adults, children, college graduates, people with only a grammar-school education, can get spiritual benefit. No sermon should in its general drift float over the heads of the audience, yet the preacher will bear in mind the cultural and aesthetic hunger of some in his audience, and on their account make use of expressions and allusions which others in the same audience are unable to appreciate. The preacher who sermonizes with only one element of his audience in view is following the line of least resistance, and this is not a courageous thing to do. He would discover, if he introduced matter into his sermons for the special benefit of the children in his audience, that many an adult would be particularly attracted by what was offered to the child.

5. WHEN THE MINISTER DOES NOT REMEMBER NAMES AND FACES

If ever the minister is tempted to play pretender, or to act a lie, it is when people, meeting him, confidently expect him to remember not only them but their names and various circumstances as well. Often he has a vague or partial recollection of the persons accosting him, and he thinks all he needs to bring clearer recollection is a little more time. So, why not pretend he remembers, then trust to luck that he will either recall more as the conversation proceeds, or that the talk will carry on and end without his being detected?

A large and varied experience teaches the minister that it is always best to confess frankly that he does not remember. To be sure, he will by such confession offend some sensitive persons. But, for one thing, this kind are not of much consequence as far as the Kingdom's work enters into consideration and their ruffled feelings will do the cause no particular harm. In the long run his candid honestly will win respect. Moreover, he can by tactful attentions later atone in most cases for the offense taken.

The minister meets many people if he is the minister he should be. In a church of six hundred he has as many people to meet, and he does not see them daily. They have only one minister. They see and hear him every time they attend their church. It is at least six hundred times easier for them to remember him than for him to remember them; and they, if they exercise common sense, will know this.

Not every case of failure to remember names and faces is pardonable, however. The minister who is truly interested in people should remember them. The minister who faithfully shepherds his flock will be in their homes repeatedly and, sympathetically attentive to even trifling circumstances and conditions in these homes, will have little difficulty with his recollection. The minister who "hasn't time" to make calls in the homes of his church members unless there is a specific need is missing some of his choicest opportunities to shepherd souls. A social call often opens doors into people's hearts and lives where the true minister should enter. Every family has something important for him to learn, important at least to that family and the souls of those who compose it.

6. WHEN THE MINISTER IS APPROACHED BY MEMBERS OF ANOTHER PARISH

Long as the Church has existed, it still has members, some of them prominent, who treat the pastorate of their congregation as though it were a position to be bargained for. They, as said before, talk of hiring a minister. Before they hire him they want to sample. He is asked to visit their church on a designated Sunday to let them hear and "try" him. What is a minister to do when he is so approached?

I am tempted to answer that the best thing for him to do under such circumstances is to say, either openly to those approaching him, or somewhere within himself where they will not hear it, but where it will be perfectly distinct to himself, "Get thee behind me, Satan!"

The grapevine is a remarkable growth. It flourishes in church circles as rankly as anywhere else. You may think you can prudently deal with people who so approach you, but your own parish members will soon be in possession of the news by the mysterious grapevine. What will they think of you and of the sincerity of your attachment to them when they learn that you have been "bargaining" with another church? What will they think and say if you have agreed to give the other church a sample of yourself and your preaching, and then are left on the bargain table unsold? Do you not see that the situation is "loaded with dynamite"? While you are saying, "Get thee behind me, Satan!" down inside yourself, the wise thing to say to the interviewers is, "I have nothing to say in such matters unless and until I have an open, written call in my hands; and what I would do if openly and heartily called I do not now know."

You need, in your ministry, all the comfort and encouragement you can possibly get. You are certain of getting it if you always bear in mind that you are in the Ministry by God's call, and that God does not call ministers by methods current in the world and its deals.

There are other circumstances under which members of a parish resort to the minister of another parish. They have fault to find with their own minister, with some of his utterances, with his position on certain questions. They want bolstering for themselves. Off they trot to waylay a neighboring minister; slyly they put questions to him, the purpose and import of which he should be shrewd enough to detect. Tell such people that you refer them to their own pastor. There are impersonal subjects and questions which you are at liberty to discuss at any time with anybody. That is different.

Another delicate situation arises when members of a parish, usually because their own pastor is in disfavor with them, apply to the minister of another parish for his services. They ask him to officiate at a baptism, a marriage, a burial, or in the sickroom. Make it your rule, when such services are asked of you, first of all to inquire whether those asking them, or those in whose behalf they are asked, are members of any parish. If they are, politely inform them that courtesy requires of you to refer them to their own minister. In the call of their parish to him they have said or implied that they, as members of his parish, are pledged to respect and honor him by having him render what spiritual services they may want. You have no call and no right to render them such services. We ministers do not belong to a closed union in which regulations as to our conduct toward one another are imposed on us; but we do belong to an honorable profession, in which we are not disposed to be discourteous to one another.

Satan sneaks pretty close when such opportunities are thrown in the minister's way. Vanity likes preferment. If the minister is nice to people under such circumstances, maybe they will presently come to swell the ranks of his own church. In other cases, I regret to say, the fee which the marriage or the funeral will yield, is enticing. Stalwart ministers in our church, having felt under exceptional conditions that they could conscientiously perform ministerial acts for members of another's parish, have been known openly to inform those who tendered the fee, "I shall give this to your own minister—I have been acting in his place." Those were brave men. That meant not only parting with needed money: it meant administering as bitter a dose as conceivable to the runaway church member.

It stands to reason that all this does not apply if the pastor in question has the consent of the other pastor when he serves his people; but even then there should be an admonition administered to the disaffected person or persons as to the obligation to one's own minister.

7.   WHEN THE MINISTER HEARS GOSSIP ABOUT A BROTHER MINISTER

Any little mar or smudge, of whatever color (it need not be black), shows more easily on a white surface than on any other. A slight defect in a diamond is more serious than a huge defect in a lump of coal. Similarly, faults and flaws in the gospel minister attract serious attention most easily.

When you were a boy, you probably liked to throw stones. It was no fun unless the stones were thrown at something. The fun reached its climax when a stone hit something. It was more fun to hit something that could either be knocked down or smashed to pieces than to hit a post or a tree. There are thousands of grownups, both men and women, who still share the stone-throwing boy's glee. It has been said that death loves a shining mark. That death-dealing activity called slander also takes pleasure in a shining mark. Slandering a vagabond is no fun, but to slander the preacher seems to be a heap of fun.

"Thou shalt not bear false witness." Would it be doing violence to God's intent when He gave this commandment, if we gave it an interpretation which would include the command, "Thou shalt not listen to false witness"? Association with many preachers has taught me that much gossip is current among preachers about their brother preachers. It may concern their preaching, their positions on certain questions, their personal habits, their manner of dealing with their church members, their attitude as to the general work of the church body to which they belong—or anything under the sun.

"Love worketh no ill to his neighbour." Let the minister always put the best construction on his brother minister's conduct when it is criticized in his hearing. Let him discourage the busybody who is toting stories about various ministers. This busybody is usually himself a minister; for few lay people go to a minister with gossip about other ministers. I have tried to find an explanation of the proneness of ministers to absorb easily and pass along discreditable tales about their fellow ministers. I reflect that a training for the Ministry makes a man's mind critical. He is practiced in making fine distinctions, largely in the moral field. It becomes second nature with him to search and see and pass judgment.

Then there is this intensely human weakness which makes us imagine that the more faults we can find in others, the higher our own rating; and the accompanying foible that, if we can relate another's failings, our hearers will consider us morally pure ourselves.

But slander is slander, and the sins of the tongue are so damning and so damnable that the minister should shun them with especial abhorrence. Defend your brother when sly tongues are trying to slay him. To affect a sympathetic air while one is narrating the latest gossip in regard to a fellow minister makes the matter only worse. If you are sincerely sorry to learn that Brother So-and-So is said to be getting lazy, that he made a bad blunder in handling the Adult Bible Class, that his church attendance is slipping because he is preaching poor sermons, then show your regret by discouraging the gossip. But your duty does not end there. Go to the criticized brother and tell him what stories are in circulation about him. You can do this in a manner which will indicate that you want to help him. Perhaps in most cases such action on your part will be resented. No matter. Do it anyhow. Ask yourself what you would want if, without your knowledge, tales were being circulated about you.

Chapter 7

THE MINISTER'S PUBLIC RELATIONS

1. WHEN THE MINISTER DISCUSSES PUBLIC AFFAIRS

In our incomparable land free speech is indeed free. Discussion of any and all subjects is in perfect order and always in full swing. The chorus is virtually equal in number to the population, barring only those who are not yet articulate. Mere boys and girls discuss subjects far above their comprehension, and callow school children are assigned to debate on the most complex national and international questions.

The subjects discussed include persons, those who are in the public eye because of position, power or performance, no matter how prominent they may be, or how high their rank or station. Public affairs of the most far-reaching importance, and public officials from the President down to the township road commissioner are made the objects of indiscriminate utterances, usually the product of immature and uninformed minds. We talk too much here in this land of free speech.

Among the indiscreet talkers the minister is far too often the loudest. Hundreds of the cloth have come to greater or lesser grief because of their indiscreet speech. I regret to feel induced to say that the minister figures far too frequently in the ranks of those who are delivering themselves on difficult questions of public affairs.

I am thinking of that frightful period of humanity's experience called the Second World War. While our service men

122

and women were building up, maintaining and putting into action the mighty force which brought about victory for us, we stay-at-homes were earning fantastically high wages, buying bonds, and day by day making ourselves extraordinarily articulate. Among the leaders in the vast army of arm-chair generals and chiefs-of-staff were hundreds of ministers. The war would have been won with ease, ended with dispatch, and the war debt of our country kept at a negligible fraction if only this or that minister had been President of the United States or chief-of-staff of our military forces.

Aside from the fact that know-it-all talk always stirs up resentment in those who are of contrary opinion, such talk stultifies ministers right and left, day by day. But the performance was kept up unweariedly. Nor am I disposed to pardon brash ones on the plea that in anxious times men's nerves are raw and their minds jumpy. Discussion of profound political matters and of public officials is the daily occupation of a vast number of the clergy. There are so many of these cheerful kibitzers that they are available at a dime a dozen. They have a citizen's full rights. No one can question their privileges. But I make bold to submit a few sentences of caution.

For one reason or another, discussion of politics seems more likely to arouse resentful feelings than any other talk. In our land it has been practically impossible to dissociate public policy from party policy; and we have few citizens who are able, or feel inclined, to remain calm and fair-minded when the policies of their political parties are unfavorably criticized. No minister serves a church whose members are of one political party. To make the situation more precarious, both the major political parties of our country have developed rights and lefts, thus making it all the more difficult to escape antagonizing people when one condemns or champions any definite political policy or personage.

Under such circumstances, is it not best that the minister, who should not unnecessarily forfeit the good will of any souls, remain noncommittal in public on controversial political subjects? To be sure, he may bridle and maintain that as a citizen of a free country he has the inalienable right to his own political opinions, as also to their proclamation. But long ago one of the world's wisest preachers said, "All things are lawful unto me, but all things are not expedient." It is not by any stretch of argument, or of the imagination, expedient for the minister to lose people's good will for the sake of mere exercise of a liberty.

Active and vocal support of individual candidates for definite offices has brought ministers and ministerial groups to grief many times. Support of any given candidate for election should be extremely quiet and cautious. I cannot forget a time when the church forces of our city threw all their energy into efforts to elect a "reform" mayor. Our city, in both government and morality, would without question undergo a thorough cleansing if this good man were elected. But after he had been triumphantly installed in the mayor's office he proved by his ineptness and inability so total a disappointment that the church forces became a laughingstock for years.

The political ranks of our land and its various electoral divisions are full of knaves and weaklings. When honest men do get into political office, they soon discover that they need votes to carry any measure. They cannot win an inch of ground, as a rule, without the votes of the dishonest. These cannot be secured without compromise. This is why so many creations and creatures of reform movements have suffered not only inglorious defeat but downright disgrace. The ministers who have identified themselves emphatically with such movements have shared in both.

Is it hypocritical for the minister to remain silent on political questions? One can be emphatic and energetic in enunciation of the underlying principles which should rule in matters of government and administration, and equally emphatic and energetic in denouncing wrong, without aligning oneself openly with any party or candidate, and at the same time feel perfectly clear in conscience.

Enters the question, shall the minister publicly attack candidates and holders of public office? Nathan openly told David, "Thou art the man!" The Old Testament prophets again and again personally denounced rulers who were immoral in person and unrighteous in rule. Shall the present-day minister not do likewise? Shall he in his pulpit and on the floors of conventions denounce Senator Sorghum or Secretary Seck or President Prune? At his peril!

How much does he know at first hand of the questions at issue and their various associations? What makes him think that he is capable of judging intelligently, under the circumstances, or would be able to do better than the man whom he is denouncing? But, you ask, when wrong is being done, is it not for the forces of righteousness to espouse the right? And can this be done effectively without attacking the wrong and denouncing the wrongdoers? The answer seems easy; but, before it is given, another question intrudes. Can the minister, supposing he has earnestly diagnosed the situation, enter the lists as a knight-errant without endangering interests which are incomparably precious and which have been entrusted to him for safekeeping?

Suppose you were a bank messenger, sent to a depository with thousands of dollars in your trust. En route, you witness a street brawl: a ruffian, viciously beating an innocent victim. You enter the fray, taking sides, of course, against the fellow who is doing the wrong. What a cad you would be to pass on without helping the victim! When the scuffle is over, the wrongdoer has been vanquished, and the honor is yours. But then, to your consternation, you discover that the thousands entrusted to you are missing! They were not yours. They belonged to your employer. Will he ignore the loss because you helped a man who was being attacked? Suppose a minister allows his Master's most precious treasure to slip from his keeping by taking sides in political matters, usually with wonderfully good intention, but with misguided zeal.

The Old Testament prophets had direct personal revelation from God, with instructions what to do. Moreover, the Old Testament Israelite state was a theocracy, and the prophets were top-ranking officers of that theocracy. We ministers of today are, no less than they were, preachers of pure uprightness and champions of the truth, soldiers of God against all wrongdoing. But ours is a perplexing task; and in most cases our course of action must be along the lines of a fearless proclamation of the fundamental principles of the Ten Commandments, and not an attack on individual wrongdoers.

2.   When the Minister Votes

When we pride ourselves on the unique country which our fathers founded and we have continued, slowly developed, and powerfully maintained, we dare not, if we are honest, hide its many shortcomings. An inalienable right which we champion and exercise is that of choosing our own public administrators. A tragic ineptness of our political system is the muddling which we unavoidably perform when we go to the polls.

Who of us knows enough about most of the candidates whose names are on the ballots, even in our own little districts or precincts? Who can intelligently decide between candidate and candidate? What minister, although he may virtually wear a party badge, believes that his own party, when he has one, is perfect, while the opposing party or parties are a menace?

The days of voting the straight party ticket are gone for millions of voters, ministers included. But, when a citizen splits the ticket as he votes, how much clear light is there to guide him? He may be convinced that John Doe's name should be scratched, but does he know that John Doe's opponent is a better man?

These things being as they are, I hold that the regulation which the minister had better set up for himself is: to be close-mouthed as to the men whom he intends to support at the polls and the men for whom he has actually voted. After all, one of our prized privileges is the secret ballot; and one's ballot loses its secrecy when one publishes what he did with it.

Among the cautions which I consider advisable is that against open espousal of the causes of most of the new parties which recurrently form as public opinion fluctuates, and as designing men try to capitalize on the fluctuations. The minister is entitled to all the quiet thinking he wishes to exercise in regard to political candidates, but let him keep that thinking quiet.

Is the most satisfactory solution abstinence from voting? By no means! The franchise is too precious a possession to let fall into disuse; and the example which a minister sets when he unnecessarily absents himself from the polls is an inadvisable one. Vote—but keep mum.

3. When the Minister Tackles the Labor Question

It has not helped to change the terms from "Capital and Labor" to "Management and Labor." The wide disagreements continue; and, as has always been the case, the general public is the sufferer. The minister is quite naturally drawn into the debate. Issues of such vital and direct concern affect us all, because of moral and spiritual implications, the minister more than others, perhaps.

But here is a question which the average minister finds more difficult than most with which he comes in contact. Its ramifications and uncertainties are veritably limitless, betraying underlying emotions on all points. To touch it without inviting indignation and hostility from somewhere is practically impossible.

Which side is right in this gigantic struggle? Both. Which wrong? Both. There you have it. The difficulties are multiplied because on both sides there are unholy extremists who positively violate God's laws and impudently flout the rights and interests of anyone besides themselves.

The minister's danger is increased by his lack of competent study of the intricacies of each individual case. Where can he find time to study the many pertinent turns in the vast labyrinth of sociology? In a specific case of disagreement and dispute, whom is he to believe? He is confronted by diametrically conflicting statements. Which are reliable? If he is to sit as arbiter, on what evidence is he to base his decision?

Taking all aspects of the general situation and of any specific contest into consideration, one thing stands out stark and plain: the minister, unable to ignore the question, must move with extraordinary caution. Whatever he says or does will be chalked up to the church's credit or discredit. It is not only his personal standing that is being risked. Wherefore let me add that he had best enter the consideration of any case with the definite knowledge of his limitations. Much as I dislike the know-it-all attitude in any minister, I positively deplore it in the minister who tackles the labor question.

Perhaps the minister's wisest course is to resort to the enunciation of the validity of the great fundamental moral requirements, and to plead with those on both sides to make sure they are playing fair and are not, in their tussle with each other, forgetting the welfare of the innocent bystander. Appeals to a sense of fairness and to the voice of conscience may not go unheeded. One often hears the profoundly impressive utterance, "There ought to be a law!" It would often be better to say, "There ought to be a gospel!"

The entire problem increases in perplexity because in both capitalist and laborer there is the inexplicable operation of the split conscience. Here is a capitalist who, in his home, in society and in the church, is a model of Christian spirit and conduct; but who, when it comes to his corporation's moves, considers ruthlessness and overreaching perfectly allowable; and here is the laborer who, in his home and in the circle of his neighbors, is the nicest kind of amiable companion, honest to a penny in all his dealings, but who in a labor riot will apparently with good conscience throw a bomb or set an incendiary fire or savagely attack the men whom he calls scabs. What can the minister do but stand aghast at such—shall I call it schizothymia? He can do nothing but wonder—and plead.

The church itself can immeasurably strengthen the minister's position by proving itself a true friend to families which suffer because of strained relations between employer and employed. Nor must it ever weary in attempting to rear its youth in a truly reverent understanding of right and wrong. I do not care again to digress into a lamentation or an excoriation of the tragic lack of discipline in the lives of the children and of the young people of the present generation. It seems like whistling in the wind to preach on the sources and the dangers of juvenile delinquency and to bemoan the passing of the real home. But, as for the church and its activity, it should not be beyond possibility to have it continue to be a light shining in darkness.

4. WHEN THE MINISTER IS ASKED TO PROMOTE COMMUNITY PROJECTS

The minister who is minded to confine his ministry to the group which forms his own congregation has a wrong conception of his calling and of his local position. He need not feel the compulsion of Wesley's famous utterance, "I look upon all the world as my parish"; and he may be quite clear in his differentiation of his parish and the rest of the world; but he must sooner or later recognize the claims of his community upon him not only as one of its citizens, but as a citizen who occupies a peculiarly influential position because he is a minister of Christ's gospel, and he owes Christ to everybody.

In earlier times, when in most localities perhaps parish and community were virtually identical, the minister was The Person in the community, often in the wider countryside. It was on this account that he later came to be designated as The Parson. Times and customs have changed. Parish and community, at least here in the States, are in most cases no longer identical. The parson is far from being The Person. Nevertheless, in all sorts of circles there is an unmistakable tendency on the part of believer and unbeliever, reverent and irreverent, to place the minister into a class by himself; a natural acceptance of the impression that the minister should be respected. With some people this gives rise to an inclination to consult him on any and every subject; with others to the instinctive refraining from saying "Dammit!" in his presence. Between these two tendencies there are various stages, all of which betoken that Christ's ministers have a definite rating in the people's estimation.

Now looms the community with its various interests and movements. It has political activities, schools, a library, a lecture course, a Y or two, a Union Aid, the Red Cross, a P. T. A., and a community club perhaps. Nothing can be more interesting than these various features of community life, even in a small village. In addition to these, there are all sorts of short-lived movements, varying from time to time. Nor is the strictly rural pastorate exempt, the difference being that in its case more territory is to be covered.

So far, so good. Why can the minister not display a sincere interest in any or all of these branches of community expression and take an active part in promoting their programs? Yet, the situations into which citizenship in a community places him can become most perplexing. Community institutions and movements often show lamentable lack of balance. The people who are willing to devote time and energy to them are in far too many cases shallow-minded, though well meaning, enthusiasts. They are at the same time sensitive creatures (the males as well as the females), and self-willed planners and plotters. The "climbers" are not unrepresented among them, and people who have set their hearts on "climbing" are not content with simply climbing higher than others, but in climbing on and over others.

So, community activities carry in themselves many of the

virtues as also many of the weaknesses of the members of
the community, and it requires an amount of wisdom and
of caution on the minister's part to shoulder his share of the
work without breaking his back (and his neck) in the transaction. Mr. A. of the Baptist Church thinks thus and so. Mrs. B.
of the Methodist Church thinks positively differently. Who of
the two disputants is right? Perhaps Mr. A. has gone as far
as to make it plain that he considers Mrs. B. an ignoramus.
Mrs. B. has gone equally far in making it plain that she considers Mr. A. an old fool. Perhaps they are both right in their
opinions of each other; but can any minister, of whatever
denomination, safely enter the situation as umpire or arbiter?

Moreover, cases arise in which the minister himself must
be either conscience-bound or guided by enlightened and experienced reason and take a definite stand which may be
seriously unpopular. To him life means considerations to
which the average person, though a church member, does not
attach grave importance. To him the morals of the community
mean more than its business progress and its alleged superiority, especially emphasized because of an old-time rivalry with
a neighboring community. To him the young people of the
community mean the future of civilization rather than objects
of pride and candidates for preferment, as planned by doting
parents. So he is bound to be, on one question after another,
at odds with prevailing notions.

Shall liquor sales be permitted in the town? If so, at what
hours? Shall the theater be open on Sunday afternoons? Shall
dances be arranged by the schools? What kind of literature
shall be displayed and sold? Shall a cheap "carnival" be
licensed to provide doubtful entertainment for a week in summer, with its irresponsible personnel and its power to draw
undesirables into the village night after night? Shall every
type and degree of gambling be rigidly, ruthlessly and impartially suppressed? Would a curfew ordinance be desirable?
What about Sunday operation of various businesses—the filling station, the candy shop, the soda parlor? There is a mul-

titude of such questions which put the minister, eager to be a benefactor of his community, "on the spot." They become painfully perplexing when they assume forms like this: "Mrs. Doe, a widow, depends largely on what her little bake and candy shop yields on Sundays; surely, she should not be required to close." But, if the minister does not object to her doing business on the Lord's Day, what of the butcher, who likes to accommodate early Sunday morning customers who either "forgot" on Saturday, or have no refrigeration?

Look at the school question. There is fairly general opinion that the educational world has gone "haywire." Young heads are being filled with all sorts of philosophies by our educators, and their hearts and consciences are being utterly ignored or completely secularized. Erratic theories are being exalted; common sense is being flouted. By example and in lectures, personal purity is being belittled by scholarly teachers. And this is called up-to-date education. If the minister interferes, he is told that Church and State are separate in our land. What to do when leading spirits in the community unite to effect reform?

Probably the minister's wisest course is to influence members of his parish in favor of his views. They can take a hand openly, where often he cannot do this prudently. After all, school principals and superintendents come and go, educational flashes wax and wane, but the families of the community and the church persist. The wise course for the minister is to make his influence for solid community uplift operative through Mr. and Mrs. Main Street. Above all else, let him beware of using community activity as a springboard for his own personal popularity.

5.   When the Minister Is Asked to Fill a Questionnaire

Nobody is disposed to deny that a minister gets a mass of annoying mail. He cannot safely toss any of it into the wastebasket unopened, because, as surely as he does, he will meet

a brother preacher who proudly shows him a book bargain or
an office gadget he has just bought. "Who told you about
this?" "Why, I got a circular advertising it about two weeks
ago. Didn't you get it?" Well, it was in the one envelope
which this annoyed preacher tossed away without taking note
of its contents.

Among the sheets reaching the minister by mail which are
most exasperating are questionnaires. They irritate the minister for several reasons. Who has the right to cross-examine
him on this, that and the other? To give answers of value he
would have to use precious time searching either his files or
his library. What's the hurry, anyhow? This can wait. And
the outcome is that the questionnaire is neglected until the
deadline of its usefulness has passed. What the statistics
actually reveal I do not know; but it is safe to hazard an estimate that, when a few dozen or a few hundred questionnaire
blanks are sent to preachers, fewer than 60 per cent of them
are filled and returned.

There may be some questionnaires sent out whose origina-
tors are crackpots, or, at best, impractical enthusiasts; but by
and large, questionnaires are circulated with some real purpose. For most ministers the time comes when they themselves
are on committees which, in order to do their work intelligently and successfully, find a questionnaire indispensable. It
is then that the negligent minister himself begins to deplore
the unresponsive attitude of his disinterested fellows.

Let him make it his invariable rule, when he receives a
questionnaire, to subject it to careful scrutiny and study.
Unless he finds, on mature reflection, that there is some good
reason for not filling it, he should by all means furnish the
information desired. Church officers, even the often ridiculed
church statisticians, are at least worthy of consideration. They
will rarely incur the expense of sending out blanks without
ample justification for the procedure.

I take for granted that, when the sender of the blank
promises that information furnished will be treated as con-

fidential, or when the minister who provides information asks
that it be so treated, the promise and the wish will be sacredly
respected. If you have reason to doubt the trustworthiness of
the man who asks you to answer questions, ignore his questionnaire. It must be admitted that breaches of confidence are
not unknown in church circles.

A questionnaire which in my opinion deserves special attention is that sent out by the theological student or the young
preacher when he is preparing a thesis and needs the help of
experienced ministers. This young man has complimented you
by sending his questionnaire. He does not claim to be self-
reliant; and he seems to believe that you know many of the
things which he has not yet discovered. Help him.

Other inquiries which merit prompt and discriminating attention are those sent by civil and military authorities. Religious statistics as compiled by the government are of im-
mense value. Their worth could be vastly increased if the
negligence of ministers in filling blanks did not deprive the
statistics of completeness. Do not raise the cry of separation
of Church and State when the State, acknowledging the incomparable worth of the Church, seeks to be of service in a
perfectly permissible way.

6. WHEN THE MINISTER DISLIKES A RESOLUTION OF HIS CHURCH BODY

It has often seemed to me that the minister is the slowest
mortal in the world to learn that the majority rules; or the
most stubborn when a resolution is adopted to which he has
been opposed. Indignant, he vows (sometimes, fortunately,
only to himself) that he will "get even." All sorts of dark
schemes may flit through his mind. The resolution is, of
course, senseless. It will hurt the church. It is simply ruinous.

Then why was it adopted? Is it wise, even though history
bears some proofs that the majority can be wrong, to insist
that one knows better than the majority? Is it not possible to

be mistaken, no matter how cocksure one is of the correctness of his position?

Better fall in line, Brother. Even if you are right, the only one in step, it is better to let time prove that, as it inevitably will, than to incur people's ill opinion by refusing to yield. It is not a question of principle, you know, otherwise it would not have been submitted to a vote. Be a conformist on matters of policy and method. If you have not enough grace of God in your heart to support the resolution cordially, at least be polite enough to remain quiet about it. Later, when time has proved that you were right, do not exult, "I told you so!" You can afford to be magnanimous and not celebrate your triumph.

Furthermore, you have the right to try to effect a reversal of the pertinent resolution. Since your church body is democratic, you dare enjoy the distinction of supporting an adopted resolution by acquiescence and compliance while at the same time you endeavor to secure its repeal. Remember that a resolution on a practical question is never worth enough to warrant the disturbance of the peace of the church.

Worse, perhaps, than open rebellion is pouting, refusing to play. It is worse, because no man can pout without suffering reactions injurious to himself. Cheer up! You did not have your way; but the end of the world and the doom of the church have not come. Have the good sense to await your vindication.

Later, you may discover that you were wrong after all. How will you feel then if you have done a lot of protesting and threatening?

7. When the Minister Leaves a Parish

Jests galore have been uttered and circulated at the expense of the minister who is about to leave one parish to enter another. Such jests might well cease. One of the minister's hardest tests comes when he receives an appointment or a

call which would send him into a new field. To be sure, let it
be reiterated, he has vast advantages over men in other oc-
cupations under the same circumstances. He enters his new
surroundings not faced by the difficulties of establishing his
social status or his business credit. He would not be entering
the new field if it had not been taken for granted that he is
socially worthy and financially trustworthy. Here is one of the
advantages of being in the Ministry of which the average
minister is too seldom mindful and for which he usually forgets to be thankful. Yet, these advantages do not relieve him
of certain serious responsibilities in regard to which many a
transferred minister has been hurtfully careless.

Leaving a parish should mean leaving it—and letting it
alone! Few ministers have the tact and good sense needed to
remain guiltless of reprehensible blunders in their conduct
toward the members of a parish which they have left. Be it
added that this is not at all astonishing, considering sentimental attachments which develop between pastor and parishioners. Both find it unnatural to sunder the ties which have
bound them together.

"Out of sight" is rarely "out of mind" as to the pastor and
the people who have parted from each other. The pastor feels
the urge to stay in touch. He is still interested in what he
built up, and he fears that his successor may not be doing just
what should be done for this or that member. Is it not his
duty to offer advice? May it not become his duty earnestly to
criticize actions (or inaction) of his successor? Indeed, should
conscientious solicitude for souls whom he has lovingly served
for some years not prompt him to take a hand in the selection
of his successor?

Temptations of this kind do not all arise only within himself. One day a couple from his former congregation come to
his new home and ask him, for auld lang syne, to perform
their marriage ceremony. Another day a letter comes, telling
him that the new minister is doing thus and so or neglecting
this and that, and asking him either to interfere or to give

advice. Again, a telegram reaches him, saying that an old parish friend has died and that the family want him to conduct the funeral service. A young couple whom he married about a year before he left are blessed with a babe, and they write and ask him to come back and baptize it. What to do under such and similar circumstances?

I have but one answer. Precious as are the friendships which develop when one serves people as their pastor, lasting as these friendships should properly be, a minister who leaves a parish should leave it and let it and all its members alone as far as pastoral services are involved. Harm inevitably comes if this course is not followed. There will be cases in which the new minister will have no objections, will even welcome his predecessor's advice and his occasional return to assist in pastoral services. Even then the utmost discretion should be practiced by the former pastor.

As for his keeping in frequent and close contact with his former parishioners by writing letters, sending birthday and other anniversary greetings and gifts, it is best for him to be very sparing in such attentions. Most of these people can be made to comprehend that this attitude on his part is best. Those who cannot will be either the vain or the unduly sensitive; and the feelings of neither are important enough to place regard for them ahead of the welfare of the Kingdom.

Occasional voluntary visits to one's former parish cannot be summarily disapproved, but they should not be frequent. When they are made, the visitor's care not to say or to do what is malapropos should be meticulous. This often makes such visits trials rather than pleasures. Every parish has its troublemakers, and a visit on the part of a former minister is their grand opportunity to exercise their officious and loquacious bent.

Infractions of the rules of proper procedure when the minister has left a parish are not obviated when he religiously keeps hands off, but has his wife maintain the relationships.

Then there is a temptation of an entirely different nature

which assails the minister who is leaving a parish. The suggestion arises, whether he should not help his successor by passing over to him various items of information on this and that parish member. There are some of these members who smoothly "took him in" before he had made their real acquaintance. Will it not be a kindness to warn his brother against them? Why let him, innocent lamb, be deceived by these wolves in sheep's clothing? But this is not the departing minister's responsibility; this alone should be the answer. If he needs more persuasion to make him keep his hands off, let him bear in mind that he "got along" happily with members with whom his own predecessor had all sorts of disagreement; and that members with whom his predecessor was on almost too intimate terms he found to be hinderers rather than helpers in the work. Church members react differently to different ministers. We of the clergy receive similar training and are supposed all to have the same ends in view. But we are personally of different types, and human nature evidences itself variously in us. Better not "tip off" your successor. If he is at all worthy to be in the Ministry, he will manage to find his way through.

Should the departing minister try to "get even" as to an unfairness which he has experienced in the parish? Is it ethical for him to utilize his farewell sermon to tell some tough sinners in his flock just what he and God think of them? Positively not! Indeed, my own practice always was not to make my last sermon as pastor of a parish a farewell sermon. Let it be a last sermon, not a valedictory. Good-byes are properly individual. When you leave, give the flock the very best gospel sermon they have ever heard from you. Valedictory sermons are likely to become very sentimental and emotional; and the preacher is in danger of being weakest and shallowest when his own person gets too prominently into the foreground of his discourse.

The departing minister should not leave a mass of unpaid bills behind him. Difficult as it may have been for him to "make ends meet" by reason of his modest stipend and the many demands his family's position made on his slender financial resources, it is a damaging thing to have it truthfully said of him, "He left town owing everybody." Some arrangement should be open to him to clean the slate before he goes. Consultation with the officers of the parish or of his church body may help; for both the parish and the church body may suffer through gossip which feeds on an unfortunate minister's financial misfortune.

May we take for granted that the departing minister has the parish records in apple-pie order? They should at all times be open for inspection and should be found faultless; but many a minister has been known, for reasons too numerous to mention and too poor to be valid, to neglect posting the records promptly. Be that as it may, leaving these records correctly and fully posted to date is a must for the minister who is leaving a parish. No excuses!

It is almost equally important that the departing family leave the parsonage and its grounds in clean and tidy condition. I have found, in visits to several hundred parsonages, that most (not all) shepherdesses are careful, cleanly housekeepers. Whether they habitually are or not, it is unpardonable to leave the parsonage "in a mess." This is long remembered by the parish women.

8. WHEN THE MINISTER RETIRES

If any creature emphatically needs a double portion of wisdom from on high, it is the minister who has retired. I do not mean the minister who, having married money or fallen heir to it, smartly retires at fifty-five or sixty, and actively leads a life of leisure; but the minister who has served until failure of health and strength makes it unwise for him to try to continue in a pastorate. I am not here discussing his pension or his support by his children. It is his conduct that has me worried.

When he remains within the area of the last church served, what a thorn in the flesh he can be for his successor! Whether or not there has been an element in the parish which had wearied of him and is thankful that a new leader has supplanted him, he still has many friends. These feel for him in his loss of position, and usually a considerable number consider that an injustice has been done to him, either by the dissatisfaction which helped to effect his retirement or by the meagerness of the pension which he receives. Their readiness to champion him cannot fail to hurt the new minister. He is made to feel like an intruder. When individual official acts are required, as for marriages and funerals, the old minister is asked to officiate solo or to have an honored share in the ceremonies. He is consulted on all sorts of questions, the decisions of which belong to the new minister. When the new minister displeases members by some utterance or some line of action or policy, the grievance is carried to the retired pastor. And so forth.

This is where the need of abundant grace becomes evident: grace enough to move the retired minister to say of his successor with inflexible determination, "He is your pastor, I am not." Indeed, he should efface himself completely from any activity in the ministry of his former church members unless and until invited by his successor. I know that close ties between him and many of his parishioners were woven, the complete breaking of which seems almost barbarous. Nevertheless, they must be broken in so far as the relationship of pastor and parishioner comes into consideration.

For this reason it is best for a retired minister to remove from his last parish. Circumstances sometimes make this impracticable. When they do, he should set his face like flint against any and every trespass on the rights of his successor. With determined firmness he should make people understand that he is out of office as far as they are concerned. No offense taken because of his attitude can equal in destructiveness the harm which arises through the interference of a retired minister in his successor's work. I go as far as to say that, when the retired minister has removed elsewhere, his visits to friends in his former parish should be very few. It will be best, too, for him not to carry on regular personal correspondence with any of his former parishioners.

What to do with his time? This will vary. Surely, he can find something with which to occupy his days. Let him apply his remaining capabilities in making himself useful in his circle. Consecrated humility should enable him to prevent himself from becoming an undesirable either in his community, or in his church circle. If he has spent a lifetime in the Ministry without learning to be humble and to efface or subordinate himself, it would seem that he has had an unfruitful ministry. The retired minister can be a model of dignified loving and lovable manhood. On the other hand, he can easily strengthen the derision for the Ministry which is sometimes evidenced in cartoons, and wit-and-humor columns.

Will he be asked to supply pulpits? I hope so. When he is so invited, what an opportunity to show how experience in the Ministry can teach a man to reach people's hearts, and to reach them without making a sermon long and wearisome! What an opportunity to weave thoughts into the sermon which will heighten people's regard for their regular minister and increase their appreciation of what the minister endures and accomplishes! What an opportunity to display one's imperishable spiritual youth and one's practical up-to-dateness!

Chapter 8

THE MINISTER'S HABITS

1. WHEN THE MINISTER BUYS BOOKS

It would be difficult, in our times, to find a minister who is not a habitual reader. "Reading maketh a full man," said Lord Bacon centuries ago. The minister knows that he dares not be empty. He must have something to carry to his people, and he needs new supplies week by week. His reading habit is one of his best.

Some ministers buy many books. Others buy few. Some ministers read many books. Others, few. Some are always buying the latest theological publications. Others prefer to stock up as they can with old stand-by "authorities." Be this as it may, every minister does buy books. Let me add that thousands buy books foolishly. I shall add the acknowledgment that the average minister is at a complete disadvantage when buying. What and who shall guide him?

He reads a review of a new book in his favorite magazine. Is the review reliable? In hundreds of cases it is not. This is very frank talk but it is truth. What the correct proportion is cannot be exactly stated; but many reviews are largely "build-ups." For one reason or another the reviewer is kind-hearted rather than a clear thinker and fair-minded. One book after another, highly lauded in the review, proves to be a sad disappointment.

142

A ministerial friend has bought a new book and goes into raptures over it. Why? Often not because he is honestly enthusiastic. There is that in us mortals which induces us, when we have spent money on something, to aver that it is superlatively good. Forsooth, shall we admit that we have made a poor investment?

Another element must be reckoned with. The average book buyer is not a competent book critic. Go slow in following the other sheep over the wall. If time and money were not so precious in the average minister's economy, careless buying would not be so serious. As it is, every transaction should be made as nearly foolproof as possible. Perhaps a few "Don'ts" will help.

Don't buy a new book (even this one) although many are raving about it. What's the hurry? You have managed without that book until now. You will not perish and you will not be outdistanced in the race for success if you worry along for a few more weeks or months without it. Wait until the book has stood the test of a little time.

Don't feel ashamed to say, when you are asked whether you have read this or that new publication, that you have not.

Don't hazard a purchase on the strength of what one reviewer has written. Compare review with review, and so get a composite estimate of the book.

Don't read reviews without seeking in them for admissions, for "damnation by faint praise." Often more is written into a book review than a cursory reading reveals.

Don't rely upon pithy excerpts from reviews, culled and printed by publishers to advertise books. A sentence or two taken out of the context in even an unfavorable review will make the book "sound good."

Is the minister who rejoices in the size of his book collection still with us? I fear he is. Somehow, he feels that a showy library is a dependable recommendation. It awes the naïve parishioner, does it not? It is something to talk about—how

many hundreds of volumes he has, how many hundreds of
dollars have gone into it. But, Brother, that kind of prestige
does not mean a thing. I do not know a single minister whose
worth is judged by the extent of his library. Nor do I know
one solidly successful minister who makes a point of trying to
impress people with his many books.

When a minister buys books, he will naturally follow certain
lines. He has his theological hobby, and he is in danger of
making that hobby a single-track device. The minister, because his work leads in so many different directions, has a
better chance to have variety in reading matter than has the
man in any other profession. He should try to keep his library
fairly well balanced. This means that he should buy some
books, the reading of which will be a task for him instead of
an easy delight. What ails many a minister is that he is ignoring those parting words dinned at him by the seminary dean:
"Now, Young Man, leaving the seminary does not mean that
your school days are over." We have far too few scholars in
the Ministry, and far too few discriminating students among
its voracious readers.

In the general run of parsonages, the book-buying minister
will have to do careful budgeting. Many rightful demands are
made on his slender income. He dare not slight the household
allowance because he is a bookworm; nor dare he forget his
intellectual requirement because he loves his wife and children and a pleasantly furnished home. He will probably never
have enough money to buy all the books he thinks he should
have. This means that reliable guidance is needed when he
buys.

What has been said here in regard to books applies equally
to magazines and other periodicals. They are a prime necessity, but their selection calls for much discrimination. Aside
from the good money that is often sunk into less valuable
current literature, there is the immensely important consideration of investing priceless time in poor reading matter.

2. WHEN THE MINISTER EATS AND DRINKS

Is there any exercise in which the human being is more prone to exhibit the animal coarseness of his make-up than in eating and drinking? We are accustomed to refer to these as the satisfying of our creature comforts. It is by God's ordinance that we must eat and drink. More than that, I am prepared to assert that God wants us to enjoy eating and drinking. He has had pictures drawn in His Revelation, the Holy Scriptures, portraying scenes in the New Jerusalem. He says that there we shall feast. There are to be trees in the Holy City which will bear edible fruit every month. A consecrated poet gives us these lines about heaven:

> *There is the throne of David,*
> *And there, from care released,*
> *The song of them that triumph,*
> *The shout of them that feast.*

Jesus speaks of enjoying the fruit of the vine. He taught us to pray, "Give us this day our daily bread." Of Him we read, "The Son of Man came, eating and drinking." All of this strengthens me in my belief that our animal side is not in itself base, and that there need be no apology for our appeasement of natural appetites. Eating and drinking, if we so determine, can be made perfectly refined.

Yet, how few there are who have cultivated table manners! In the rearing of children continual effort is necessary to keep them from making pigs of themselves. Few people emerge into manhood (Shall I venture to add womanhood?) able, or even inclined, to be refined while they are eating their meals. College life and seminary life in most institutions do not contribute to the polishing of table deportment. The college has provided one of the picturesque phrases of our language, that striking expression, "Boardinghouse reach." Boys at college seldom have (or take) time to be real gentlemen at their meals. Presently they are in the Ministry, and they have brought with them their boardinghouse liberties and crudeness.

But why worry about this? Let me tell you. In my own experience as head of a district of more than two hundred churches, required to recommend pastors to vacant churches, I at one time proposed a very able minister to a church whose pastorate any man might well be happy to secure. The minister whom I recommended happened to be making a journey which took him through the city in which this church was located. He was induced to stop over and meet a few members of the church's official board. One of these entertained him in his home as a dinner guest. After that time this minister was determinedly ignored by the officers who were acting as the pulpit committee. Why? Simply because his table manners were atrocious. To say the least, I was dumbfounded, knowing the man's fine qualifications; but a few years later I happened to be at table with him at a convention, and I soon saw—and was fully convinced. He was "terrible." No other word will do.

I knew a clergyman who was serving as head of one of our higher schools. For a celebration a group of his students, girls and boys, were dining at an inn, with the teaching staff present. Arrived at table, the minister in question picked up the napkin placed at his plate, tossed it into the center of the table, and announced so as to be heard by all, "We don't use these at home, and I'll not use one here!" Imagine!

Shrug your shoulders and pooh-pooh if you will: the fact remains that there is a difference between a pig and a gentleman; and no ability or scholarliness entitles a minister to be a pig. People have a right to look for a degree of personal polish in the man whom they elevate to the position of leader and example for themselves and their children. What excuse is there for a minister's ignoring the generally accepted canons of table etiquette? Admitting that some of the accepted rules of polite table etiquette are arbitrary, refined society has, for one reason or another, accepted them. The

most talented minister has no license to defy them, and he
does so at his peril. Emily Post has been made the butt of
many jests, especially on the part of ministers. Just the same,
she knows.

Why insist on passing food to one's mouth on the tip of
one's table knife? Why insist on buttering, then spreading
with jelly or jam a whole slice of bread unbroken, then biting
into it at the risk of daubing one's ears? Why insist on leaving
one's spoon in one's cup after stirring one's coffee or tea? Why
reach across the table or past one's neighbor at the right or
the left instead of asking for what one wants or waiting until
it is properly passed? Why grow impatient before the first
course is served and begin eating bread or rolls or salad or
relish? Why lay one's knife or fork (often both are so laid)
slanted from the edge of one's plate to the table? Why eat as
though one were ravenously hungry? All the infractions of
table etiquette are evidences of a lack of restraint; and the
minister, above all others, should be able and happy to practice restraint.

If he were only willing to consider, and to take himself in
hand, he would by better table manners obviate one of the
chief reasons why he cannot hold the loyalty of the young
people in his parish. They, especially the girls, will be slow
to overlook infractions of etiquette, no matter what admirable
traits the minister may have.

What applies to actions at meals applies equally to table
conversation. The hearty guffaw, out of place for the minister
anywhere, is doubly intolerable at table. To engage in the
facetious and supposedly clever jargon in current use in the
common boardinghouse is wretched form. "Chase the cow
down this way" is not a proper substitute for "Please pass the
cream." Potatoes are not spuds in polite conversation. Wiener-
wursts are not hot dogs; doughnuts are not sinkers, when
good form is being observed. Shredded wheat is not baled
hay; eggs are not hen fruit; asparagus is not grass. Yet I have
often heard just such terms used when ministers were at

table. The use of slang is some ministers' method of trying to show that they are perfectly at ease, and "know their way around."

3. WHEN THE MINISTER SMOKES

Whatever may be your position on the debated question whether a minister may or may not with propriety use tobacco, you will have to admit this one thing, that there are many ministers who do use it. There is the reverend old minister who gets much alleged solace from his pipe. There is the lively young minister, just out of college and seminary, who cannot pass a single half hour without a few draws on a cigarette. There is the dignified, pompous, middle-aged minister who considers both pipe and cigarette out of order, but who satisfies his aesthetic taste with twenty-five cent cigars.

Never having used tobacco myself, although I spent two years in academy, four years in college, and two and one-half years in theological seminary, with most of my fellow students smokers, and have been in the Ministry sixty-four years among strong-smoking ministers, I hesitate to discuss the tobacco habit. I trust those who read these lines will believe me when I say that I can discuss the subject dispassionately. I am not a "crank" in regard to the minister's use of the weed.

I cannot contend that it is a sin for anyone, even a minister, to enjoy tobacco in such moderation as to make sure that it does not injuriously affect his health. But I believe that I can say, from years of observation, that either there is something in tobacco which makes its addicts careless, often slovenly; or else those who are addicted to it are constitutionally of a careless nature. I notice that the smoker seldom cares where he throws a burned match or a burning stub; that it does not matter to him where the ashes may fall; nor does he often inquire whether the smoke which he puffs into the air is offensive to others who are present. I notice that, inured from long practice to the stench of stale tobacco smoke and castoff cigar and cigarette stubs, he lets them fly and lie anywhere almost, to the disgust of those whose sense of smell has not been dulled by the introduction of tobacco into the system.

If the minister chooses to be a smoker, let him be genteel enough to be a considerate smoker. I wish he would not give me a headache and bring stinging pain to my eyes by insisting on smoking when we are having a meeting in a small room. I wish he would consider it improper to meet his parishioners with tobacco ashes streaking his coat lapels. I wish he would know that having a cigar in his lips at an angle, and keeping it there while conversing, makes him look and sound like a bum. I wish he would understand that approaching the bedside of a delicate invalid with the rotten stink of tobacco about him is inexcusable.

I wish, too, he would agree with me in the opinion that, somehow, it does not look just right for a minister to smoke while he is walking on the street; and that it is out of place for him, when he is making pastoral calls, to enter homes with a smoking cigar or cigarette in his hand, or in his mouth. Also, that there is something entirely unfit in his striking a match or snapping a lighter and starting a smoke as soon as he emerges from the church after conducting a service; or (and this happens) lighting up a smoke in the sacristy even before he emerges. I have personally known at least two ministers who smoked in their sacristies during services, one of whom said he needed a few puffs just before entering his pulpit to preach the Sunday sermon.

In the whole tobacco matter there is an underlying consideration about which I have often wondered. The minister is constantly warning his people against letting the material things gain mastery over them. Should he, then, himself indulge in the enjoyment of any material thing which so masters him that he simply cannot remain without its use for even a short time? Should a minister, who, of course, preaches self-control to the young people of his flock, allow an appetite or a craving to become habitually so strong in himself that he gets nervous and irritable if it is not appeased at regular short intervals? Many a minister cannot sit through a synodical session of a few hours without stealing out and having a few cigarette puffs. Why not? He can sit through the session without food or drink, but not without a smoke. Why not?

For some ministers the question of health enters. Oh, the minister can easily find a physician who will tell him that the use of tobacco does not injure anyone's health. Physicians also smoke, some of them far too much. I am convinced that I have known more than one minister who allowed the use of tobacco to reduce his efficiency, even to shorten his life, by undermining his health. Then, at the funeral, the officiating pastor said piously, "Since it hath pleased Almighty God, in His wise providence, to take out of this world the soul of our departed brother."

It is beside the mark to trot out the example of the old resident who was a hard smoker from his boyhood but lived to be ninety, as also of the total abstainer who died at thirty. The question is not whether there are exceptional constitutions which can successfully resist the deleterious effects of the immoderate use of tobacco, nor whether there are other causes which can undermine health and bring death. The question is, What is the use of tobacco doing to your nature, your habits, your reputation and your health?

4. WHEN THE MINISTER FINDS FAULT

One of the widely adopted outlets for human discontent is finding fault. The minister is often subject to spells of discontent. Being human, he can easily become a faultfinder. Moreover, one of the Devil's schemes to deceive men is imbuing them with the idea that finding flaws in others is proof of their own superiority. Because the critic in various lines has honorable standing, the faultfinder proudly fancies that in reality he is an accomplished critic, not an ordinary grouch.

There are, as I have pointed out, ministers who habitually

censure the Ministry itself, their brethren in the Ministry, the general church bodies and their officers, and for good measure various members of their parishes. The parsonage, the church edifice, the organ, the location, all are mediocre. There are ministers who follow the great American indoor and outdoor sport of criticizing our government and all its incumbents. All of this would be bad enough if they kept their gripes hidden. But disapproving is not fun unless one can parade it; and far too many ministers keep theirs on constant display.

Seeing defects, and expressing one's feelings in regard to them, are two different activities. Naturally, the minister sees and hears much which, he discerns, is not as it should be. Naturally, he also feels the responsibility of trying to better imperfect conditions. But the way for him to live up to his insights and duties is emphatically not to make himself an inveterate carper.

Here is an opportunity for the exercise of consummate wisdom and skill. What a pity that it is so seldom tactfully grasped! No amount of excellence in other respects will save the minister who becomes known as a habitual detractor. Faultfinding is in deserved disrepute and contempt. When I read what Paul wrote to Timothy in regard to the characteristics which a preacher should have, I cannot help thinking that in some of the terms which he used ("no striker . . . patient . . . not a brawler") he was thinking of the censorious preacher.

Probably the worst specimen of ministerial faultfinding is that which crops out in the preacher's sermons. I think there is often an unexpressed restiveness anyhow in the hearts of church members, when they are expected to sit unresisting while the minister is preaching, with not a chance to talk back. This becomes an unendurable experience when he repeatedly scolds and denounces in his sermons.

Almost equally offensive is the habit of some ministers of finding fault with their wives when they are out in company together. What is reprehensible enough when done in the privacy of the home becomes an outrage when done in public. Belittling one's wife is not a way of gaining prestige in the Ministry. But let me, to be fair, express equal disapproval of the minister's wife who publicly calls attention to her husband's failings. She is not a *rara avis*.

In conclusion, what shall we think of the minister who, attending another minister's church service, goes there with sharpened pencil instead of a whetted appetite for spiritual food?

5. WHEN THE MINISTER FISHES FOR COMPLIMENTS

It is pretty hard for a man who is walking along the bank of a stream with a rod in his hand, on which is fastened a line, at the end of which is a hook, on the point of which is bait, to avoid giving the onlooker (a game warden?) the impression that he intends to fish. If only the minister knew that he is not fooling anyone except himself when he tries without being suspected to evoke compliments concerning his work! Commendation is so delectable a morsel, and condemnation is so often the minister's reward instead, that we might be inclined to pardon him when he takes rod, line and hook in hand in quest of words of praise.

Just the same, it is as unwise a proceeding as he can well devise. Praise is worth exactly nothing when it is sought intentionally; and seeking praise is so transparent an operation that the least observing person can readily see through it.

Some ministers do not even try to conceal their thirst for praise. "What did you think of my sermon last Sunday?" "How do you like the way I conduct the Bible Class?" "Did you hear me on the radio this morning?" "Did your boy say anything about the pep talk I gave the Sunday School a week ago?" "What did your husband think about the talk I gave at Kiwanis week before last?" So it goes. And the Master never said anything more solemnly than the words, "He that humbleth himself shall be exalted," and "Whosoever exalteth himself shall be abased."

But, suppose admirers do come and praise the minister for this and that. Shall he hush them? He need not. But, when they have brought him a sizable fish, he need not grab for more and bigger ones. And he had best, without intending any underestimation of his friends' good intentions, not place too high a valuation on any spoken praise.

I have noticed that the minister who bids for compliments is the same one who falls into the error of overestimating himself; and he often goes on to the development of a pride and arrogance which not only do not befit the minister but often lead to his fall. It is almost inevitable for the minister who overestimates his worth to begin to rest on his laurels. "What lack I yet?" he asks, self-satisfied. Presently he finds himself sadly discounted. If there is any calling in which a man needs constantly to be trying to improve, it is the Holy Ministry. Woe to the minister who begins to imagine that he has reached perfection and need no longer strive!

6. When the Minister Envies a Brother Minister

Brother minister seems to be more successful; and this brings about one of the most trying situations for the ordinary minister. Did he not sacrifice and slave to be able to enter the Ministry? Does not God owe it to him to crown his efforts with phenomenal success? But here is his neighbor, or his conference brother, or some other minister of his acquaintance, apparently "playing rings around" him. That brother is attracting notable attention as a pulpiteer, increasing his church membership year after year by dozens, even by fifties, having his salary increased periodically, while he himself is "getting nowhere" noticeably. It is not easy to hold still and keep sweet in the face of all this.

Brother, if haply this means you, stop and think. Why do you suppose you were once told the fable of the race between the hare and the tortoise? Bah—only a fable! Just the same, the outcome of many a race has been that same reversal.

Remember that the Scripture says that all which is required of stewards is that they be found faithful. Make sure that you are truly faithful, and leave the rest with God. I say, make sure. Maybe you have not so diligently and prudently capitalized on your abilities as you should have. Replace your discomfiture with introspection. Ask some friend for a diagnosis.

Next, bear in mind that not all fields are alike. You may be scratching in stony soil of low production, while your more successful brother is tilling easy soil. Moreover (and this is highly worth considering), scratching in that stony soil, "pecking on a rock," as it were, may be exactly what you need to develop your latent talents for glorious use in the future.

Lives of great men all remind us
We can make our lives sublime.

How many of history's great characters began their careers with discouragement and apparent failure!

Will it be unwise for me to add the old maxim, "Appearances deceive"? I do not want you to cultivate envy by questioning whether your brother's apparently extraordinary success is partly sham. God's Word is replete with warnings against that dread enemy called envy. But the maxim remains true; and it applies to so many cases in the Ministry that you are entitled to a crumb of comfort from its consideration.

7.   When the Minister Has a Hot Temper

The minister who is incapable of feeling and displaying moral indignation is not worth much. Supine acceptance of unrighteous conditions and practices is not wholesome for any society. Old-time preaching abounded in outbursts of righteous wrath and definitely plain talk. Some of its vehemence was probably uncalled for, but, on the whole, it benefited.

Outbursts of hot temper are something else. There is a real difference between holy indignation and ordinary anger. The minister has a right to get angry; and, again, it is wrong for him to be angry—according to the character of his wrath. St. James writes: "Let every man be swift to hear, slow to speak, slow to wrath: for the wrath of man worketh not the right-eousness of God." That designation, "every man," includes the minister. He enjoys no special dispensation granting him the liberty of letting his temper get the best of him. Somehow, his loss of temper is more hurtful to him than other men's loss of temper is to them; and, certainly, nobody has ever gained by the experience.

No diet so sadly affects a man as to have to eat his own words. Hot-tempered individuals always get their good share of this diet. Since the minister is by profession a man of words on which often people lay much stress, it is a double trouble when in rage he allows his words to explode to do him discredit.

The hot-tempered minister does more than let fly regrettable words. I knew a clerical synodical official who, in a conference, slapped a brother minister with whose position he disagreed. I knew another pastor who, in anger, chased a boy out of the Sunday School—and lost that boy's family. I have known more than one to lose the respect of their brothers in heated discussions on convention floors.

The most dangerous kind of temper is that which, instead of blazing and then cooling, continues to glow. It is that which prompts some ministers to make open, personal attacks from the pulpit on church members, or to say nasty sarcastic things about them or to them in conversation. Some ministers go into print "with their dander up." Theological controversy in book and magazine has often contained accusations and implications so harsh and bitter, and so far from being really true, that they have bordered on the slanderous, or even gone across the border. Small wonder that, far from edifying the lay reader, such controversy has discredited the Ministry and at the same time increased people's indifference to religious truth.

"What's home for, anyhow?" questioned the boy who, observing polite restrictions when he was visiting, let himself loose in his own home. What I think of the minister who makes his wife and children the targets of his explosions of anger had best not be set forth here at any length. I despise a man, still more deeply a minister, who can contain his temper away from home, then erupts on the heads and feelings of his family. He is, by the way, only deceiving himself when he imagines that he can confine knowledge of such inhumanity to the home circle. "Murder will out." I have known more than one parsonage wife whom church members have profoundly pitied because she had to live "with that kind of man."

What to do when one is in the Ministry and has an ungovernable temper? Just one thing: "Ye must be born again." Do not feign Nicodemus' astonishment. No matter what the temperature of your enkindled wrath is, God's grace is sufficient to control it. But you will have to possess that grace. If you do not, what are you doing in the Ministry, in which you constantly proclaim its merits?

Suppose, now, that God's grace did not operate promptly, and the minister's temper has led to a real quarrel. Ministers are so human that they not only go as far as to quarrel, but they often quarrel very seriously and vehemently. A minister may quarrel with a brother minister, a church officer, his church organist, his wife, or a neighbor. Following the usual pattern, the minister's quarrels generally arise from some trifling disagreement.

Waiving any discussion of the ins and outs of a quarrel's development, the question is, What shall the minister do when he has had one? There is but one answer; and it must be plainly set forth and underscored, because in numberless cases ministers have not done their Christian duty after having quarreled. I perhaps need not remind them what the Scrip-

tures tell sinners to do under the circumstances; but I fear
we ministers do need to be reminded that we above all others
should possess and display enough Christlikeness to do the
godly thing after such sinning.

Often the minister dignifies, or tries to dignify, his quarrel-
ing by wanting it considered zeal for a correct opinion or position. Often it seems as though he were trying to justify himself
by saying that he is a graduate of college and seminary, well
read, ordained, and hence must be right; and that plainly the
fault of any quarrel between him and another must clearly
be the other's fault. What a commentary on his supposed
Christlike humility! Did Jesus have the ministers of all ages
in mind when He told Peter, "Not seven times, but seventy
times seven"?

Quarrels should be settled and canceled promptly. Not
only that: every time the minister needs to "kiss and make
up" with someone, he should strengthen his resolve not to
quarrel again, no matter how provocative the circumstances
may become. "A soft answer turneth away wrath." Is there
any situation in which a man of God cannot give a soft
answer?

8.   When the Minister Slips into "Gross" Sin

Before *The Scarlet Letter* was written, and since that time,
there have been cases of ministers' falling a prey to the tempter
and making themselves guilty of "gross" sin. Before the bar
of God's justice every sin is damnable. In men's judgment
many a sinner who, under stress of peculiar temptation in an
hour of peculiar weakness, falls into gross sin may at heart be
a better person than another who practices the "lesser" sins
again and again, perhaps continuously. Shall we permit a distinction between gross sin and lesser sin? The distinction is
generally accepted; and when a minister falls into what is
almost unanimously termed gross sin, we must face a situation
which has its many perplexing points.

We correctly teach that a repentant sinner, no matter if his sin be mass murder, finds forgiveness in the Cross of Christ by the mercy of God. Though the minister, by reason of his stewardship of the holiest things, is adjudged a greater sinner than others when he does fall, God's wide mercy surely embraces him when he, in spite of the supposed special strength which he possesses, becomes weak enough to let the tempter ignominiously overpower him. If he truly repents, his sin is covered, his transgression is forgiven: the Lord does not impute his iniquity to him. David covered this ground experientially in the Thirty-second Psalm.

The question is whether the forgiven gross-sinning minister should remain in the Holy Ministry. There have been those who maintained that a man, after falling into gross outward sin, then repenting, has all the greater power to preach the forgiving love of God and the cleansing atonement of Jesus. They have pointed to the conversion from dissolute or profane life of men who then became powerful evangelists.

Others have claimed that a preacher who has yielded to gross temptation has so grievously besmirched the holy calling that he should voluntarily eschew all thought of serving any longer as a minister or should be ecclesiastically deprived of any right to continue in the Ministry. Still others have suggested that he, in case of true repentance, should be sent to distant parts where his fall would not be known, there to go on with his service.

It is not to the credit of the Church that often in such sad cases a considerable difference has been made in the treatment of offenders. The gifted "successful" minister has often been accorded much more lenient treatment than the mediocre. One hears that it would not only be a pity but a distinct loss to terminate the able man's service; and for this reason some way must be discovered or devised to conserve his usefulness in the Ministry.

Weighing all the arguments, and having been officially in sorry contact with cases of the kind, my conviction is that the offender should of his own accord demit the holy office. While there are those who will excuse and forget, there are more who cannot. The constantly alert, observant and vocal multitude of those who, while not scoffers of God and of holy things, are caustic and ready critics of the Ministry and the Church, find too much ground for protest when a minister goes far astray from the path of decency. Allusion to powerful evangelists who before their conversion were notorious sinners is malapropos. They did not commit their gross sins while in the Ministry.

The erring minister need not try to comfort himself by thinking he can escape in strange territory the nauseous odor which his weakness or willfullness has originated. Knowledge of sin of this kind has a way of following the perpetrator from place to place, no matter how remote the region. "Be sure your sin will find you out!" Comes the added question, when church officers devise a scheme by which the minister under consideration is transferred to a new field, what can be said when those in the new field learn, as they eventually will, what has been done to them?

Note how careful Paul the apostle was and urged his fellow ministers to be. "Giving no offence in any thing, that the Ministry be not blamed." If baleful blame could assail the Ministry when its incumbents erred slightly, how can we expect it to withstand the shock when they err grossly?

Demitting the Ministry may not be sufficient if the fallen minister is earnestly desirous of making all possible amends for the injury which he has inflicted on his calling. It may be necessary for him to remove entirely from the scene of his downfall. While his sin may, as we say, follow him, it will not elsewhere create much disturbance, provided he no longer claims a right to occupy the Ministry. Renunciation is one of the most potent methods of disarming carping critics and regaining the respect of offended friends. The more the renunciation includes, the more sincere it will seem to be.

After he has renounced, the self-unfrocked minister should

remain so repentant that he will not indulge in flings and quips at other ministers who give evidence of weakness, errors of judgment and little deviations from strict uprightness in their work. I have profound pity for the minister who has strayed into gross outward sin; but I have no patience with the spirit which prompts a man to say, "Well, I caught it: let me see how uncomfortable I can make it for someone else." Misery has always loved companionship; but misery of this kind has no right to try to force others into its company.

This discussion cannot close without words of warning to the minister who has not fallen into great transgression. "Let him that thinketh he standeth take heed lest he fall." It might be wise for him occasionally to take his Bible concordance and read devoutly and with serious introspection the many passages which say, "Take heed!" It might be wise, too, to give psychological study to the probable reason why his brother strayed into adultery or slipped into intemperate drinking or acquired the narcotic habit. It might be wise frequently to take inventory of one's own "besetting" weaknesses. "Let us lay aside every weight, and the sin which doth so easily beset us." James Moffatt renders it, "Strip off sin with its clinging folds." Luther made it read, "Sin, which always sticks to us." That term, "besetting sin," calls for frequent contemplation.

This discussion, the hardest in the book, has been most reluctantly written. I have set these opinions down, mindful of the warning, "Considering thyself, lest thou also be tempted." God have mercy on us all!

9. WHEN THE MINISTER GROWS OLD

"Thou shalt rise up before the hoary head." So speaks Scripture; and, as always, it speaks well and wisely. This same Scripture, however, nowhere says, "Hoary Head, thou shalt demand reverence because of thy whiteness." The phenomenon of the minister who presumes upon the respect due to

his age is not an exceptional one. You may not agree; but it is
my opinion that the self-satisfaction of the older minister has
been one of the chief contributions to the disinclination of
parishes to extend calls to men over forty-five and fifty years
of age.

I advise the minister with all his art and determination to
fight against aging physically, mentally, and in disposition.
The care of the bodily self is a prime obligation. Too many
ministers take too little physical exercise. Too many smoke too
much. Too many have ruinous dietary habits. Some of them
sleep too little. Some of them, always telling their parishioners
not to worry, fret too much themselves. Too few of them observe regulations which would insure steady nerves.

In the same strain let me add that too many ministers indulge in self-pity. One hears them tell how much work they
have, how tired they are, how little time they have, what a lot
of trouble certain persons have caused them, and how exasperating certain members of their parishes are. They make
life miserable for their families, and fritter away their own
physical endurance, an asset they can ill afford to squander.

As the minister grows older, he must, to hold his own, remain mentally alive and alert. No minister has ever reached
the point after which mental growth was not necessary. It is
a constantly changing humanity with which the minister has
to deal, and in whose interests he exists and labors. If he is
stagnant mentally, he will soon find himself only tolerated.
On the fundamental articles of his faith he has a right to be
inexorably conservative. On all else he had better cultivate
the habit of changing his mind.

Too many ministers make themselves believe (Do they
really succeed?) that satisfaction with their own conclusions
and a conviction that these are always wise and right are
actually beneficial conservatism. You hear them making
apodictic statements on all sorts of subjects. The older they
grow, the more positive they are. The contrary should be their
practice: the older they have grown, the more astonishing

reversals of accepted truth they have witnessed, the more careful they should be to reach conclusions slowly and to keep such conclusions fluid.

The aging minister dare not become careless about his clothes, his hair, his hats, his shoes and his cravats. He must not let a stoop gain possession of his shoulders or a rasp get into his voice. Physical culture, if begun early enough and practiced conscientiously, will make it possible for him to keep a spring in his step and a sweep in his stride for years and years. He should also continue developing a spirit which easily allows him at least one hearty laugh every day, preferably five or six.

He should not allow himself to become cynical as the years increase. Cynicism is not wholesome philosophy, nor is it a mark of spiritual-mindedness. Neither is it an evidence of wisdom, or superiority of intellect and judgment. Making faces at others' youthful enthusiasms does not make old age or old ministers beautiful.

One of the best tonics, or, let me say, one of the best regular diets for the minister whose age is advancing is as much association as possible with young people, and, in such association, appreciation of their spirit and point of view. I am about willing to say that the aging minister should pay reverent deference to the spirit of youth. One reason which parishes advance when expressing their preference for a young minister as pastor is that he will do better work among the youth. The discreet old minister can easily make this preference look very silly. He need only give young people the credit and admiration they deserve.

The aging minister can also spring a genuine surprise on his audiences by speaking briefly. Age does not, as many an aging minister seems to assume, confer the privilege of extending the length of one's sermons. At the same time, his battle against pulpit mannerisms should grow in determination. It is true that, even if he gets careless, there will be some of his friends who will say, "Oh, good old Dr. Doe is

peculiar in many of his ways, but we love him just the same."
The more peculiar he gets, the oftener they will feel con-
strained to say it—proof sufficient that they and he are on a
losing defensive.

Making reminiscences a large part of their conversation is
one of the weaknesses of which older ministers are guilty,
and through which they become bores. They live too patently
in the past. What interests most people and what really matters above all else is the present with its urgent problems.
The minister who lives in the past, and does so in a way
which indicates that he wants his people to live there with
him, makes himself a nuisance.

To the end of his days the minister should remain humble.
Age brings with it an accentuation of the deplorable habit of
wanting to recount one's accomplishments. Rehearsals of one's
own prowess and successes do not interest many listeners, nor
advance the old minister's chances of being continued in his
ministry by a satisfied parish.

Chapter 9

THE MINISTER'S MOODS

1.   WHEN THE MINISTER HAS "RISEN FROM THE RANKS"

"All men are created equal," declares our Declaration of
Independence; and therein it expresses a truth so precious
that men should be willing, as long as the world stands, to
die for it. But this does not mean that in the continuation of
the human family some do not enter life with advantages
which others do not at their birth possess. Background, after
all, means something.

"He rose from the ranks" is an expression used in the military service. Hundreds of ministers have "risen from the
ranks." Some have come from what are called very humble
surroundings. Some have emerged from disreputable homes,
their fathers and mothers being destitute of what we com-
monly call character.

Viewing our various origins, we in the Ministry should
often take thought concerning ourselves. In our letters home,
and our visits there, do we perhaps assume airs of superiority
over relatives and acquaintances? Nothing is more unbecom-
ing; and, in cases in which humble parents have made painful
sacrifices in order to get their boys educated for the Ministry,
nothing could be more contemptibly ungrateful. It may be a
little awkward for the minister, visiting his boyhood haunts,
to avoid a condescending attitude and to refrain from using
expressions which hurt; but—do it!

Here is another pitfall. I have known many ministers who have carried far into the Ministry some of the crudeness of early surroundings. I have known one or two who gloried in not having refined themselves of its marks. With all due acknowledgment of the shallowness and hypocrisy of much that is classed as refinement, and of many people who are superficially polished, the church minister should be a refined gentleman. In dress, manner and speech, he should avoid all that suggests coarseness. Even in his everyday habiliments he should be presentable, unless briefly engaged in work about the place which requires working clothes. He should shave every day.

Shoes, linen, handkerchief, all these should bear inspection. His hair should never be unkempt, fingernails never in mourning. And with all this care, he should never enter the "stuffed-shirt" class.

There is a third danger which haunts the minister who has "risen from the ranks." Sometimes he bears with him, unable to overcome it, a sense of inferiority. No one can value humility in the Ministry more than I do. Yet I advise the minister never to feel inferior to other men or to other ministers except in the sense in which the Scripture tells us that, after we have done our utmost to be faithful to our trust, we should always in God's sight consider ourselves unprofitable servants, and "in honor preferring one another." For us to feel a sense of helplessness in the presence of wealthy people, successful businessmen or witty lawyers is not creditable to us, no matter how humble our origin, no matter how many poor relations we have. We are ambassadors of The King. If He considers us fit to wear His livery, who are men, that we should tremble in their presence?

One of the assets of the Ministry is that it has carried into its composite the experiences and bents of all sorts and conditions of men. I see no particular advantage in a minister's being able to say that for many a generation his forefathers have worn the cloth. Many a man whose father, grandfather and great-grandfather before him were ministers has been outshone by the minister whose dad was a humble gardener, small merchant, or common laborer.

2. WHEN THE MINISTER ENJOYS SPORTS

The sound-mind-in-a-sound-body theory necessarily carries with it cultivation in both college and seminary of a liking for sports; there is something astonishingly persistent in an inclination to baseball, football, hockey, la crosse, tennis, or basketball. Only a very few solemn, abnormal souls still disapprove of the liking for sports which prevails in student circles.

This liking carries over from the college into the seminary, particularly if the divinity school is a department of the university. Completion of the seminary course and entrance into the Ministry finds at least nine out of every ten ministers still thorough "fans" or "bugs" or "nuts" on sports. The young fellows in a parish hail ministers who used to "play short" on the college nine, were well known "sluggers," had the record of pitching a row of no-hit games, were high-class forward-passers, or never failed to make the extra point after a touchdown. They gather around any minister who was athletic, and still is. His record in sports means more to them than his theology.

Will he sin if he maintains his interest in sports? Shall he organize a ball team, captain it, pitch or field for it? Shall he frequent the stadium and the ball park and be a lusty "rooter"? Shall he keep posted on all the transfers of players in the big and the minor leagues?

It seems to me that he should exercise cautious moderation in this regard. Athletics is one thing, professional sport is another; and so many disreputable things and persons are connected with the latter that the minister should not too deeply involve himself in the sport world. He may attend ball games, but not so often as to cause comment. He may foster athletics among the people of his parish, but should always remain duly decorous. Noise and banter, which so often accompany a game, should not find him enlisted. Nor should he devote much time to reading the sports news. Of actual news there is not a great amount. Of so-called "dope" there is; and most of it is only "dope," nothing more.

The question of Sunday ball games intrudes. A legalistic spirit in regard to Sunday observance is, I believe, discountenanced by most ministers today. They seem to have come to an understanding that there was much in the required observance of "God's Day" in the Old Testament that was ceremonial law only, not moral law. Most of us no longer observe the seventh day of the week. In Christian liberty we have chosen the first day of the week. We do not observe the regulation as to a Sabbath Day's journey. But, surely, we must all acknowledge that the Lord's Day should have a distinctive character and dress, and that these are not adequately supplied by setting aside an hour or two for worship and edification within the walls of a church edifice, the remainder of the day to be hilarious, noisy and worldly. Sunday ball is a noisy exhibition. It differs greatly from a quiet private game of tennis or croquet on one's own lawn. I do not like to see the minister so "sporty" that he cannot remain away from the baseball park on a Sunday afternoon, all his protestations of innocence notwithstanding.

It has always seemed to me that he should also definitely refuse to be interested in prize fighting. To call the fights of today exhibitions of The Manly Art is a bald deception. How ministers of the gospel of Christ can get all keyed up about two men who enter a roped-in enclosure to see which can "knock the other out," how they can get absorbed in the bruised flesh and blackened eyes of the fight ring, is difficult for me to comprehend. Perhaps I am dense.

3. WHEN THE MINISTER JESTS

"A little nonsense now and then is relished by the best of men." This being true, and the minister being one of "the best of men," it follows that he will, at least now and then, enjoy a little nonsense. It is to be hoped that he has learned early that nonsense is one of the trickiest exercises in which people engage.

Certainly, the minister does not want to be an unsmiling, dry-as-dust individual. But, on the other hand, he does not want to be a buffoon, and he should not risk creating the impression that he does not look at life, his own and other people's, seriously. This is precisely where the use of nonsense in conversation proves tricky. It is as difficult to remain exactly within the line which fixes the permissible amount of nonsense as to judge where and when nonsense is entirely out of order. More than this—it may be harmless to engage in nonsense in a certain church member's presence when this member is in one mood, but not at all pardonable when he happens to be in a different frame of mind, as is often the case.

The minister had better exercise extreme caution in being "a good fellow." He had better feel his way at all times, and rather subject himself to the criticism of being too sober than to that of being too frivolous.

Not only should he select the times for jesting very cautiously, but he should be meticulously careful in his selection of the jests, quips and humorous anecdotes which he tells. The ones who at all times engage in relating funny stories very often dip into the suggestive and salacious for the special regalement of their hearers. I regret that I must feel compelled to warn men of the cloth against telling smutty stories, whether broad or veiled. Such stories should be so obnoxious to the minister (Is he not the man of God?) that he is known neither to employ them nor to show anything but distaste when they are used by others in his presence.

I feel extremely embarrassed in admitting that I have known ministers who told dirty stories with apparent relish. I feel almost equally embarrassed in admitting that I have known lay members to take particular delight in purveying such filth in the presence of ministers, and were well rewarded for their impudence by eliciting from some ministers apparently hearty enjoyment. These were ministers who were afraid they might be considered dull or dense if they did not "see the point." A suggestive story should not win so much as a faint smile from any minister. One may not feel in position to rebuke the panderer of smut publicly, but can abash him quite effectively by showing disgust.

There is a type of jest which is called the "practical joke," largely indulged in at school and college. Some people consider it immensely clever. Let the minister keep himself clear from any participation in it. A practical joke is seldom perpetrated without inflicting a hurt, and the hurt often leaves a scar which shows for a long time. The minister will do well not to trifle with sensitive feelings in this way.

One of the valid objections to certain kinds of jokes is that they do not register unless someone in the company is made their butt. They need a victim in order to be a success. There is also the minister who in public makes his wife the butt of frequent jests, seeming to think himself highly accomplished. This is not only cheap—it is detestable. The minister may imagine that it "makes a hit"; but I am telling him that it very decidedly lowers his church members' opinion of him.

What of jests in the pulpit? There is a clear line of distinction between jests and amusing anecdotes. No minister has a right to introduce a mere jest into his sermon. He has a perfect right to employ an amusing anecdote when it aptly illustrates a point he is trying to make clear. Humor can lend itself effectively to the preaching of both faith and morals. But its proper use in a sermon is an art which few preachers master; and, unless one can master it, he had better not attempt its practice. To tell a funny story in the pulpit merely for the sake of giving the sermon some wanted brightening or seasoning, or for the purpose of getting advertisement as an interesting speaker, is to lay oneself open to well-merited, unfavorable criticism.

Some preachers feel that they cannot possibly show the right interest in children without acting childish in their contacts with them. They realize that the child has a claim on the minister, and to satisfy this claim they often make clowns of themselves to win the child's admiration. At other times they treat the child as though it were still in the cradle and needed to be tickled under its chin. Naturally, then, "kiddish" jests are in order. Careful! This child is a great deal deeper than you guess. Make it feel quite at ease in your presence, but use better judgment in your conversation with it. Silly jests are not the proper agency to dispel a child's uneasiness (often only imagined) in the minister's presence; nor are they a particularly impressive method of convincing parents that he is "*so* unselfishly interested in children."

There are certain subjects on which the minister should never jest. One of them is Marriage, a subject on which numberless inept and demoralizing jokes have been fabricated. Another is Sin. Too many souls, as it is, make light of this damning blight. Still another is the Hereafter, Heaven and Hell. To talk lightly of difficulties which certain souls supposedly have had in getting past St. Peter at the pearly gates is in abominable taste and is wretched guidance. The old chestnut, used by the minister who smokes, that he would rather smoke here than hereafter, is a sample of the trifling which some ministers think it clever to use in dealing with an awful subject.

Little patience as I have with the minister who seldom smiles, and committed as I am to the practice of wanting at least one good laugh every day, I nevertheless take a firm stand against the "horse laugh." Good breeding, still more ministerial propriety, disapprove the clergyman whose laugh can be heard "away across the hall." Misguided man—he thinks such a laugh is the hallmark of a genuine human being!

4. WHEN THE MINISTER HAS THE BLUES

Everybody gets them. The minister of the joyous, life-sustaining gospel of Jesus is no exception. Abraham, Moses and Elijah got them. Jeremiah had them so persistently that blue moods are still called Jeremiads. Do not be surprised if they occasionally overtake you. The only thing to watch is your conduct while they envelop you. In my opinion, the greatest danger when the blues take possession is that the minister may cultivate the habit of self-pity. Once that has become a fairly fixed habit, he is in danger of becoming an unmitigated nuisance. The emotion of pity is not bestowed on us for "home consumption."

It is the young minister who rides nearest to the verge of contracting this silly habit. He has made sacrifices, many of them, and has spent years of time and effort in preparing himself for a calling concerning which he has cherished glorious visions. Oh yes! he has observed that many a minister did not seem to be clothed with radiant sheen of joy in service. But that, in the student's judgment, was the minister's fault. He had evidently lost his enthusiasm.

For this young minister to discover, when he has barely begun the shining career of Kingdom service, that this service brings with it constant experiences of disillusionment, for him to bump into the deadening lack of appreciation and co-operation which seems to be the main stock-in-trade not only of the average church member but also of the average church officer, is so severe a shock that self-pity immediately gets at least the toe of one foot inside the young minister's door.

He had received so inviting a call to this attractive parish that his elation in the presence of his less fortunate classmates was almost sinful. Can he now believe the testimony of his own senses? Did he really understand the vestrymen when they gingerly tabled a suggestion from him which meant daring progress? Was devout, pious Mrs. Praywell actually in earnest when she said she would have to reduce her subscription because a few of her chickens had been stolen?

Young Man, before you have a good cry, ask yourself whether you have been a good strategist by bouncing on your vestrymen and your church members in general with optimistic plans and programs of your own conception which you know have not been tried out. The one thing neither buoyant intentions nor careful seminary training can do is to make an immature young candidate mature. Only time and experience can do that. Do not misunderstand me. I love young ministers. I admire so many of their traits and ways that I hope never to be too "sot" in my own ways to get inspiration and new vigor by observing them. What I mean is stop grieving and make a fair investigation of the reasons for your failure before letting the blues have their way with you. Self-pity will give you more trouble in the long run than all the indifferent church officers and obstreperous church members your parish can possibly contain. It has a way of sapping your manhood and making a wretch of you. Millions of women are today wearing men's garb. Don't let self-pity put you into petticoats.

Further, if you just cannot keep up enough optimism to escape the blues, do not make your wife and family miserable because you feel down in the mouth. Your wife has enough to tax her patience and fortitude. She has troubles with which she, plucky little soul, never troubles you. She is always telling the children, "Now, don't disturb Papa!" Play fair with her. By all means let her help you in your difficulties. A feminine hand can often brush formidable obstacles out of the path. But, when you lean on your wife for help, let it be one brave soldier looking to an equally brave comrade for reinforcement, not a fleeing coward asking a comrade to cover his retreat.

As for your children, you have always proclaimed that you expect at least two of your boys to enter the Ministry. What impression will they get of the Ministry if the minister with whom they have constant association lets the Ministry make a "sour puss" of him? I say again, if you cannot deny the blues occasional visits at least deny them the right to talk out loud in the presence of your children.

As for your church members, you are risking their confidence in you as a leader and a strong counsellor if you let them discover that the gospel which you preach and the Captain whom you champion have not the power to keep you out of the doldrums. You know this without my telling you, unless you are one of the pathetic souls who enjoy having the attention of sentimental church members. You have heard of the woman who "enjoyed" poor health for years?

Here is a recommended technique for banishing the blues. Whether you have a Metropolitan Opera voice or not, cultivate the habit of singing: not lustily trumpeting a song over the neighborhood, but quietly, *sotto voce,* singing the comfort of some grand old hymn into your heart. This procedure can chase the Blues Devil most efficiently. I would daily, preferably early in the morning, do enough singing of this kind to keep him at a distance. Then you need not drive him away.

But, underlying all this should be a happy trust and an abiding heart-joy in Jesus, who is the Author and Finisher of our faith to an extent which makes faith "the victory that overcometh." After all, the white gladness of companionship with Christ does not belong with the blues. "Scrouge closer" to that marvelous Cross of Calvary. That is where the minister belongs when he has the blues—and when he does not have them.

5. When the Minister Thinks He Is Going Stale

The self-conceited minister (and he is by no means a rare specimen) never worries about himself. Why should he? His sermons are above par every week. His handling of every

situation into which his duties carry him is so superb that he
revels in relating to less able ministers (meaning all the
rest) how adroitly he handled this condition and that person.
His voice is just right, his manner above criticism. His ways
are model.

Not so the humble self-inspecting minister. After every sermon he asks himself whether he should not and could not
have done better. If he were to preach it again, could he not
improve it in this respect, or another? Did he spend as much
time and attention on its preparation as he should and might
have done?

He is equally critical of himself in regard to the application
of his time day by day; to his manner in making pastoral calls;
to his dealings with the young people of his flock; to his conduct in the sickroom; to his attitude in the face of opposition;
to his feeling when disappointments come. "That the man of
God may be [not imagine he is] perfect, thoroughly furnished
unto all good works." That pattern, set for every child of God,
he believes is specially applicable to himself in the Ministry.
And oh, how far short he falls of its inviting perfection!

Well and good! But in steps the danger that he may let
wholesome self-inspection degenerate into morbid hopeless-
ness. He is going stale, isn't he? He has reached the end of
his usefulness in his field, hasn't he? He broods; and the longer
he broods, the worse his situation seems to grow. What shall
we advise?

First of all, that he rid himself of the feeling that he has
done all in his field that he can blessedly do. Admitting that
there are only a few more souls who might be gathered in,
admitting that he can do little or nothing with certain members whose good will he has irretrievably lost, he has no valid
reason for thinking and saying, "My work in this field is
done." The real work of winning souls, of edifying God's people, of building the Kingdom of Christ by applying the Word
which is "given by inspiration of God, and is profitable for
doctrine, for reproof, for correction, for instruction in right-

eousness," is here to be done. The discouraged minister is
not the man to judge whether he or another can do it best.
If there is really nothing more for him to do in this field, will
there be anything for a successor to do?

Many a discouraged minister's worries arise from the circumstance that there are certain lines of his service which he
likes better than others, in which he is convinced that he
excels; and, when a field no longer gives him opportunity to
"shine" in his favorite capacity, he thinks he has gone stale.
A pretty safe prescription for him to write for himself is that
he take up with genuine assiduity other lines of operation.
He may then soon emerge from his gloom, wondering why he
ever imagined there would be nothing more for him to do
unless he were given a new field.

Or, Brother, do you think you have gone stale simply
because the report of your parish at the end of the year did
not provide sensational statistical reading? Are you again forgetting that your main work is the erection of structures in
the inner man, invisible to the eye, eluding the cold analysis
of the professional statistician? Bear this in mind.

Unable and unwilling to pry into your inner life, do not
call it ungracious of me to advise you to ask yourself whether
you are in close daily contact with the great Upper Shepherd
of souls. I shall not say that you should perhaps devote more
attention to prayer in your own behalf; for I fear you might
interpret this to mean that you should spend several hours on
your knees every day. What I mean is that many of us who
regularly admonish our people to take God by the hand and
keep Him close as a constant Companion fail ourselves to
practice the "close walk with God." It is unthinkable that any
servant in the Ministry of the Most High should ever find this
Ministry tedious and irksome, should ever go stale, if he is
keeping close to God and to Christ's Cross, in unbroken communion with them. Lift your work to a high plane, and keep
it there. Dealing with immortal souls for their temporal and

eternal salvation—how can it ever become a humdrum occupation?

You may occasionally need a tonic. God knew, when He established the "office of reconciliation," that He could best administer this office through human agency. God knows that you in His Ministry, no matter how well you have identified yourself with Him, will often need the tonic of human encouragement and guidance. You should have a close friend, preferably a minister and one of a different disposition from your own, to whom to go, sometimes as to a confessor, sometimes as to a confidant. It is for us ministers to pay close heed to the Scripture admonition, "Bear ye one another's burdens, and so fulfil the law of Christ."

6.   When the Minister Feels He Is a Misfit

Although the old adage, "A rolling stone gathers no moss," is still in good standing, no one condemns the man who once was in the grocery business but now is a prosperous real estate broker, or the woman who prepared herself for the teaching profession but now is high up in the personnel department of some big corporation.

It is different in the case of the minister. "Once a minister, always a minister" has fixed itself in people's minds. The Roman Catholic Communion maintains that ordination for the Holy Ministry confers an indelible character on a man; and, somehow, there is prevalent in Protestant circles a feeling that something at least fairly similar happens when either by episcopal or other solemn ordination a man having taken school training for the Ministry is ceremoniously ordained for this office.

On the basis of this impression two phenomena develop. One is that the ordained minister carries about with him the conviction that he is settled for life and that the Church owes him a living. The other is that Church authorities cast about for all sorts of expedients to provide a place for the ordained

man who is obviously not fitted to his calling. But this is not
being written to consider what the Church should do when an
ordained man has so many weaknesses that no church can
profitably have him serve in its pastorate. I wish to discuss the
minister who of himself is convinced that he is a misfit in the
Ministry. What is he to do? What line of action on his part
will be least unwise?

Well, why not first of all try to discover wherein unfitness
centers? Does he have shortcomings which cannot be corrected? Most of us are poor analysts of ourselves: few of us
are honest, stern analysts of ourselves. But, although frank
advisers are not so numerous as they should be, a minister can
usually find a confidant who will, when he sees that the minister is in earnest, call his attention to his weaknesses.

Then arises the question, Can these be overcome? In many
cases they can be, even though the victory requires a long-
continued valiant struggle. Overcoming mischievous habits is
not a holiday for anyone, least of all perhaps for the one
whose youthful belief in his own supposed competence has
long since wooed him into the confidence that he is "all right."
The most difficult piece of armor to put on and get properly
adjusted when one has his own weakness to fight is humility.
It is a common observation that, despite all their denuncia-
tions of pride, many ministers lack true personal humility. The
impression that one is a misfit comes from the outside.

Unless the handicaps are attributable to a lack of mental
stability, or to physical defects which cannot be corrected,
there is no reason why they cannot by the aid of the Holy
Spirit be conquered. Even deficiency in education can be
remedied, for it is never too late to learn. Physical defects
which discount the minister's acceptableness, notably those
which affect speech, can be overcome by determined exercise.

When a minister has reached the definite conviction that he
is not fitted for the duties of his high calling, let him quietly
and without complaint seek rehabilitation for some other honorable vocation in life. To this should be added that if a

minister discovers he is not wanted anywhere in the Ministry, let him do likewise. When he does this, let him drop the "Rev." which has been prefixed to his name, try to make himself a model in whatever activity he takes up, prove a specially useful worker in the church which he joins, and, by reason of his own training for the Ministry, give the pastor of his church intelligent and sympathetic support. Someone should arise who will effectually disprove the prevailing opinion that the ex-minister is a nuisance in any church. Here is a glorious opening for the man who has in his own forum been adjudged incompetent as a minister.

7.   WHEN THE MINISTER IS CORNERED

This happens comparatively often, even to the minister who boasts that he knows all the answers. The men and women, the youth and the children with whom he has conversation of one kind or another are not dumbbells. Most of them are quite keenly observant. Add to this the strange circumstance that many people have an inclination to be specially observant of the minister, always on the lookout for any aberration from the paths of regularity and propriety, quick to notice any real or apparent weakness or insufficiency in him. It is fun to detect the minister in any shortcoming.

The minister who adds to such people's amusement by foolish attempts to extricate himself when he gets into a "tight spot" is largely responsible for his own and other ministers' discomfiture. The know-it-all attitude does not befit anyone, least of all the man of God. A frank admission of his limitations becomes him and will help avoid many conversational corners, into which he might be crowded, an uncomfortable and very ridiculous specimen.

It is both refreshing and disarming to have an educated, scholarly man say, "I do not know." And he can with all propriety say this in regard both to some religious and secular matters. There are many things which God has not revealed to us. The minister need not pretend knowledge concerning these. Many questions have two quite reasonable sides; he had better not be cocksure on either. Paul says, "We know in part . . . we look through a glass darkly." A momentary failure of memory can expose the minister to the danger of making false assertions.

One of the most embarrassing of the minister's experiences is to find himself getting into a corner while preaching. Conscientious, careful preparation of every sermon is an effectual safeguard. But what minister among us all always goes into his pulpit fully prepared and safely fortified? Again and again we find ourselves in tight corners before an audience. Even one's best friends in the audience find it difficult to be gracious enough to pardon the minister when he, after introducing a perplexing subject, contents himself with only pretending to meet the issue. Evasions in sermons are neither fair nor acceptable. The minister should beware of getting himself into a corner while he is preaching.

The danger usually arises when one, as his sermon delivery proceeds, happens to have some thought come to mind which did not occur while the sermon was in preparation. What a splendid thought it is! It must be introduced. Then comes the disaster. Brother, better leave the splendid thought invading your mind for use in some future sermon.

The minister runs another risk when, in a debate which may develop, he resorts to alert repartee to cover his position. Sallies of wit can never serve as adequate substitutes for real argument. Only a few people are diverted by them. The minister may remain in a corner after he has made his most brilliant sortie. Not only is honesty (in debate) the best policy: it is the only moral policy.

8. WHEN THE MINISTER LOSES PATIENCE

He NEVER should—PERIOD.

Index

Set in Linotype Caledonia
Format by John Rynerson
Manufactured by The Haddon Craftsmen, Inc.
Published by HARPER & BROTHERS, *New York*